Contents

Introduction

About this book

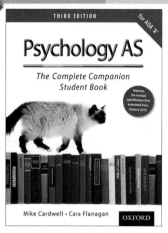

THIRD EDITION

for AQA 'A'

Psychology AS

The Complete Companion Student Book

Matches the revised specification first examined from January 2012

Mike Cardwell · Cara Flanagan

OXFORD

This book is a mini version of *Psychology AS: The Complete Companion*. It contains just the basic information needed for the AQA specification 'A' AS examination. There are no frills and no extras.

When a cook makes a special sauce he or she will boil the liquid for a long time so that it reduces in volume, leaving just the most essential (and tasty) ingredients. That's what we have done here – produced the nuggets of knowledge necessary to enable you to focus on what you *must* learn in order to do well in the exam, as distinct from what you *could* learn. In order to make the most of the material presented in this book you should use it alongside *Psychology AS: The Complete Companion* or your own AS textbook.

The book is organised as follows:

Cognitive psychology: Memory >	Subsection 1 >	Topic 1
Developmental psychology: Attachment >	Subsection 2 >	Topic 2
Research methods >		Topic 3
Biological psychology: Stress >		Topic 4
Social psychology: Social influence >		Topic 5
Individual differences: Psychopathology (abnormality) >		

The AQA specification A AS consists of 6 **modules** (or sections). These are cognitive psychology, developmental psychology, research methods, biological psychology, social psychology and individual differences.

Each module is subdivided into two **subsections**.

In this book, topics have been identified within each subsection. Each **topic** is covered on a *single page*.

In total there are a mere 49 topics!

This book starts with some details about the examination and tips for doing well in the final examination.

Introduction	>	About this book
		The AS exam
		AS exam questions
		How your answers are marked
		AS exam advice
		A mock exam

The AS exam

There are two AS exams: Unit 1 (PSYA1) and Unit 2 (PSYA2).

- In each exam all the questions will be compulsory.
- You will have 1½ hours on each paper to answer about 10 questions (some questions are parted).
- The total mark for each paper will be 72 marks.

 Unit 1

Cognitive psychology, Developmental psychology and Research Methods

The exam paper is divided into two sections, each worth 36 marks.

There will be **one** 12 mark extended writing question on this paper. Quality of written communication is assessed in this question. There may be other extended writing questions worth 6, 8 or 10 marks (all these questions require description plus evaluation in equal measure).

Section A – Cognitive psychology and Research methods

In this section you will be asked questions on the topic of memory, and also be given some brief descriptions of hypothetical studies of memory and asked research methods questions in relation to these hypothetical studies.

Section B – Developmental psychology and Research methods

In this section you will be asked questions on the topic of attachment, and again, will be asked research methods questions about hypothetical studies of attachment.

Psychologists carefully noted the pets' response to the broken water dish.

Unit 2

Biological psychology, Social psychology and Individual differences

This exam paper is divided into three sections, each worth 24 marks.

There will be at least **one** 12 mark extended writing question on this paper. There is no guarantee as to which section it will appear in. Quality of written communication is assessed in this question. There may be other extended writing questions worth 6, 8 or 10 marks.

Section A – Biological psychology

Most of the questions in this section will be on the topic of stress. About 4 marks are likely to be allocated to a question(s) on 'how science works' in relation to stress research.

Section B – Social psychology

This follows the same pattern as section A – mainly questions on the topic of social influence, but there are also likely to be about 4 marks' worth of questions on 'how science works', this time related to social influence research.

Section C – Individual differences

This also follows the same pattern as section A – mainly questions on the topic of individual differences, plus possibly 4 marks' worth of questions on 'how science works', this time related to abnormality.

How science works

The theme 'how science works' is a key feature of the Psychology examination. This includes your knowledge of the methods psychologists use when conducting research, and the advantages/limitations of these methods. It also includes the issues of reliability, validity and ethics.

In all areas of the specification you need to be prepared to answer questions related to the topic of 'how science works'.

Introduction   > About this book
                                                    The AS exam
                                                    AS exam questions
                                                    How your answers are marked
                                                    AS exam advice
                                                    A mock exam

AS exam questions

There are various types of question that you are likely to encounter.
We have examined some of the main ones here.

Question types	Example	Advice
Recognition question	Tick **two** of the boxes below to indicate which of the following are features of the working memory model. **A** Serial position curve ☐ **B** Incidental learning store ☐ **C** Central executive ☐ **D** Phonological loop ☐ *(2 marks)* AQA, January 2011 Unit 1	*Questions like this can sometimes be quite easy and sometimes quite difficult! It is worth taking extra time to make sure you have selected the right answer rather than rushing and throwing away valuable marks.* *It is worth reading the question several times and making sure you follow the instructions. Students often lose marks because they haven't followed the instructions – for example selecting three answers where only two were required. In such cases you will simply get **zero** marks.*
Short description question	Cognitive interviews have been developed to improve witness recall. Identify and explain **two** techniques used in the cognitive interview. *(3 marks + 3 marks)* AQA, June 2009 Unit 1	*The number of marks available indicates the depth required in your answer.* *The term 'identify' means 'just give a simple answer'. The term 'explain' requires further elaboration.*
	Outline the main features of the pituitary-adrenal system. *(3 marks)* AQA, January 2010 Unit 2	*Questions will relate to specific content in the specification, such as 'the cognitive interview' or 'the pituitary-adrenal system', so it is vital that you know your specification.*
	Outline what is involved in Cognitive Behavioural Therapy. *(3 marks)* AQA, January 2009 Unit 2	*Always read the questions carefully – 'what is involved' specifically asks you to describe how a therapy is done rather than asking for a definition of what it is.*
Longer description question	Outline the main features of the multi-store model. *(6 marks)* AQA, January 2009 Unit 1	*Again, the number of marks available gives you guidance about how much to write.*
	Explain how locus of control influences independent behaviour. *(4 marks)* AQA, January 2010 Unit 2	*In any description question (e.g. outline, explain) you should avoid including any evaluation, which would not be creditworthy.*
Research studies	**Questions about research studies have a number of important features**	
	'How' questions Outline how **one** research study investigated the accuracy of eyewitness testimony (EWT). *(4 marks)* AQA, January 2009 Unit 1	*Questions that say 'how' are asking for procedures only. There will be no credit for aims or findings/conclusions.*
	'Show' questions Describe what research has shown about the effect of the age of witnesses on the accuracy of eyewitness testimony. *(6 marks)* AQA, January 2010 Unit 1	*Questions that say 'show' are asking for findings and/or conclusions only.*
	'Anything goes' questions Describe **at least one** other study into misleading information. In your answer you should include details of what participants were asked to do and what results were found. *(6 marks)* AQA, June 2011 Unit 1	*In some questions both procedures and findings are creditworthy.* *There is an important difference between questions that say 'outline research' and those that say 'Outline **one** study'. The difference is that in the former case you can describe one study or several studies whereas in the latter case you will only receive credit for the details of **one** study.*

Introduction	>	About this book
		The AS exam
		AS exam questions
		How your answers are marked
		AS exam advice
		A mock exam

Differences	How does the behaviour of securely attached infants differ from that of insecurely attached infants? *(4 marks)* AQA, June 2009 Unit 1	*Credit will be given for one difference in detail or more than one difference in brief. You will only gain full credit if you actually identify the difference rather than simply defining the two terms.*
Evaluation, strengths and limitations	Evaluate the behavioural approach to psychopathology. *(4 marks)* AQA, June 2010 Unit 2	*Be guided by the number of marks available and be careful to address the specific demands of the question. In the first example strengths and/or limitations are both creditworthy. There is no requirement for a balanced answer.*
	Outline **one** limitation of the behavioural approach to psychopathology. *(2 marks)* AQA, June 2009 Unit 2	*In the second example, strengths would not be creditworthy, and writing a second limitation would also not be creditworthy.*
	Name **one** psychological method of stress management. Explain **strengths** of this method of stress management. *(1 mark + 5 marks)* AQA, June 2011 Unit 2	*In the third example only strengths are creditworthy.*
Applying knowledge	A student teacher finds it very difficult to remember pupils' names. She decides to look in a psychology book to find some useful strategies for improving her memory. Outline **one** strategy the student teacher could use, and explain why this might improve her memory for pupils' names. *(4 marks)* AQA, January 2009 Unit 1	*In these questions you will be given an everyday situation (the question 'stem') and asked to use your psychological knowledge to provide an **informed** answer. You must make sure that your answer contains psychological knowledge but at the same time you must ensure you are answering the question.*
	Outline **one** strategy the student teacher could use, and explain why this might improve her memory for pupils' names. *(4 marks)* AQA, January 2009 Unit 2	*In this question many students write about memory techniques, but don't explain how such techniques would actually be used for remembering names.*
Extended writing question	Outline and evaluate Bowlby's explanation of attachment. *(10 marks)* Outline and evaluate research into the effects of anxiety on the accuracy of eyewitness testimony. *(12 marks)* AQA, June 2009 Unit 1	*Any question worth more than 6 marks is an 'extended writing question', where there are marks for both description (AO1) and evaluation (AO2) in equal measure (i.e. 4+4, 5+5, 6+6). Occasionally a question worth 6 marks also requires description and evaluation – and will use those words to advise you about what is required.*
	'Abnormality is very difficult to define. It can be hard to decide where normal behaviour ends and abnormal behaviour begins.' Discuss **two or more** definitions of abnormality. *(12 marks)* AQA, January 2010 Unit 2	*The word 'research' refers to studies and/or explanations/theories.* *The instruction 'one or more' or 'two or more' means that if you only write about one explanation (or two definitions, etc.) you could still gain full marks.* *Quotations are meant to guide you – but remember to answer the question, not the quotation.* *In the exam answer booklet there is space to plan your answer to this important question.*
Research methods (only on Unit 1)	You will be given a description of a study and then a number of short questions such as: **a** What is the dependent variable in this study? *(2 marks)* **b** What experimental design was used in this study? *(1 mark)* **c** Explain **one** strength of this experimental design in the context of this study. *(2 marks)*	*These questions only appear on Unit 1.* *Some of the questions require **contextualisation**, i.e. you only get full credit if you apply your knowledge to the study described in the exam question. For example, for part (c) you would need to identify one strength and then say why it is a strength in **this particular study**.*
How science works (on Units 1 and 2)	Give **one** strength of using a questionnaire. *(3 marks)* Outline **one** ethical issue in this research and say how you would deal with it. *(2 marks + 2 marks)*	*On both Units 1 and 2 are questions on 'how science works', i.e. about the methods psychologists use when conducting research, the strengths and limitations of these methods as well as issues of reliability, validity and ethics. There are often questions requiring you to interpret a table or graph.*

Introduction   > About this book
                                                        The AS exam
                                                        AS exam questions
                                                        How your answers are marked
                                                        AS exam advice
                                                        A mock exam

How your answers are marked

Assessment objectives

There are three assessment objectives in AS exam questions:

AO1 Description

> For example, 'Outline the multi-store model' requires a description of the model.

AO2 Evaluation and application of knowledge

> For example, 'Give **one** strength of the multi-store model' requires you to provide some evaluation of the model.

> Or 'Suggest **two** strategies that Sanjay could use when revising' requires you to apply your knowledge.

AO3 Design, conduct and report research

> For example 'Explain why the researcher might have chosen to use a volunteer sample' requires you to demonstrate your understanding of the research process.

In general, you do not need to worry about these assessment objectives – you simply answer the exam questions.

The only time you do need to think about AO1 and AO2 is for the essay-style questions.

- These questions start with the word 'Discuss' or 'Describe and evaluate'.
- This means you need to provide description (AO1) and evaluation (AO2) in equal measure.
- These questions are worth more than other questions – perhaps 8, 10 or 12 marks.
- These questions are likely to be marked used the mark scheme shown below.

How marks are awarded

In general, marks are awarded for detail and elaboration. The main difference between a good answer and a weak answer is the amount of *detail* (in AO1 answers) and *elaboration* (in AO2 answers). See page 9 for advice on how to improve the detail and elaboration of your answers.

Abbreviated mark scheme for 12 mark questions

	Description (AO1 – assessment objective 1)		
Marks	Detail	Knowledge and understanding	Selection of appropriate material
6	Accurate and reasonably detailed	Sound	Appropriate
5–4	Less detailed but generally accurate	Relevant	Some evidence
3–2	Basic, lacks detail and may be muddled	Some relevant	Little evidence
1	Very brief/flawed	Very little	Largely or wholly inappropriate

	Evaluation (AO2 – assessment objective 2)		
Marks	Use of material	Range of issues and/or evidence	Expression of ideas, specialist terms, spelling, etc.
6	Effective use of material to address the question and provide informed commentary and evaluation	Broad range in reasonable depth or narrower range in greater depth	Clear and good range, few errors
5–4	Reasonable commentary and evaluation but material not always used effectively	Range in limited depth or narrower range in greater depth	Reasonable, some errors
3–2	Basic commentary and evaluation of research	Superficial consideration of restricted range	Lacks clarity, some specialist terms, errors
1	Rudimentary commentary and evaluation	Just discernible	Poor, few specialist terms

Introduction	>	About this book
		The AS exam
		AS exam questions
		How your answers are marked
		AS exam advice
		A mock exam

AS exam advice

Writing good answers

Detailed description

If a question says 'identify' then you know a single word or phrase will usually be sufficient for your answer. But if the question says 'describe', 'outline' or 'explain' then you must provide some further information. Consider this question and answer:

Question: 'Describe **one** reason why people obey'.

Answer: 'Because it is justified'.

The answer, so far, is only worth one mark and needs more detail to attract further credit. You could add detail by:

- **Providing an example**: 'People obey because it is justified, for example during the Holocaust, Nazi propaganda portrayed the Jews as a danger to all Germans, thus justifying the horrific obedience that was to follow'.

- **Adding a study**: 'People obey because it is justified. This was shown in Milgram's study of obedience to authority, where participants were told that science wanted to help people improve their memory through the use of reward and punishment, thus justifying their role in delivering electric shocks'.

Elaboration in essays

The main difference between a weak essay and a good essay is the amount of *detail* (AO1) and *elaboration* (for AO2).

For good elaboration you should use the **three point rule**:

1   **Identify** your AO2 point (e.g. criticism, application, individual difference, etc.).

2   **Justify** it (what evidence do you have for this?).

3   **Elaborate** it (how does this affect the topic being evaluated? Is this good or bad for it and why?).

For example, if your criticism of a study is 'lack of ecological validity' then you have identified it. You need to justify your claim in the particular study (e.g. studies of this phenomenon in other settings haven't produced the same results). Finally, you need to indicate why ecological validity is a problem in this study (e.g. this means that we can't generalise from the original study to other settings, which limits its explanatory usefulness).

Effective revision

- **Get yourself motivated** – People do better when they are highly motivated. Don't expect someone else to motivate you (the draw of £50 for exam success) ... think of your own reason why you really want to do well.

- **Revisit regularly** – Knowledge that is not used regularly becomes less immediately accessible. The trick, therefore, is to review what you have learned at regular intervals. Each time you review material, it will take less time and will pay dividends later on!

- **Short bursts are best** – As you probably know, your attention is prone to wander after a relatively short period of time. Research findings suggest that 30–45 minutes at a time is best. What should you do when your attention begins to wander? As a rule, the greater the physiological change (i.e. go for a walk rather than surfing the Internet), the more refreshed you will be when returning for your next 30–45 minute stint.

- **Be multi-sensory** – Why stick to using just one of your senses when revising? Visual learners learn best by seeing what they are learning, so make the most of text, diagrams, graphs, etc. By contrast, auditory learners learn best by listening (and talking), taking in material using their sense of hearing. You may associate more with one of these styles than the other, but actually we can make use of many different types of learning styles. As well as *reading* your notes and *looking* at pictures and diagrams, try *listening* to your notes and *talking* about topics with other people, and even *performing* some of the material such as role playing a study.

Exam stress

A moderate level of stress is good for performance but too much can impair your ability to recall information and use it effectively in the exam. A wise student learns to control their stress *before* the examination, and makes frequent use of stress management even during the revision stage.

One interesting fact is that physical activity (e.g. stretching your arms or feet) reduces stress because the activity tells the body that the stressor has been dealt with and, therefore, the sympathetic nervous system can 'stand down', putting you in a more relaxed state.

Introduction	>	About this book
		The AS exam
		AS exam questions
		How your answers are marked
		AS exam advice
		A mock exam

A mock exam

We have written two mock exams for you to try, one for each unit exam. When you have revised the content of each unit you should answer the questions under timed exam conditions. Suggested answers can be found on our website www.oxfordschoolblogs.co.uk/psychcompanion/blog/book-resources/as-mini-companion-3.

PSYA 1 Mock exam

Time allowed: 1 hour and 30 minutes.
The marks for questions are shown in brackets.
Question 10 should be answered in continuous prose.

SECTION A: COGNITIVE PSYCHOLOGY AND RESEARCH METHODS
Answer **all** questions.

1   The working memory model consists of several components, some of which are listed below.
   A   The central executive
   B   The phonological store
   C   The articulatory process
   D   The visuo-spatial sketchpad
   Copy the table below, and fill in the letter for the component which matches each description.

Description	Component
1. Modality free system which assigns tasks to other components.	
2. Acts like an inner voice, repeating words that are heard.	
3. Stores information about sounds.	
4. Used, for example, when counting how many windows there are on your house.	

(*4 marks*)

2   The multi-store model of memory was one of the first explanations suggested for how memory is organised but it is no longer considered an appropriate model for understanding memory.
   a   Explain **one** reason why the multi-store model is no longer well-respected by psychologists.   (*4 marks*)
   b   Outline **one** strength of the multi-store model.   (*2 marks*)

3   Short-term memory and long-term memory can be contrasted in terms of capacity, duration and encoding.
   a   Give a detailed description of the capacity of short-term memory.   (*3 marks*)
   b   Describe how psychologists have investigated encoding processes in memory.   (*4 marks*)
   c   Explain **one or more** problems that have been encountered when conducting such research.   (*4 marks*)

4   The primary school in a small village is located right next to the village shop. School children inevitably call in to the shop on their way home from school to buy sweets. One day, a group of 10-year-old children were in the shop when an armed raid took place. The children were interviewed separately by the police about the identity of the men who raided the shop.
   a   Explain why the children might not be good eyewitnesses. Refer to psychological research in your answer. (*3 marks*)
   b   The police decided to use elements of the cognitive interview when talking to the children. Select **one** element of the cognitive interview and explain how this might have been used with the children.   (*3 marks*)
   c   Explain why the use of this element of the cognitive interview might have been effective.   (*3 marks*)

5   A group of psychology students have been studying strategies to improve memory and decide to conduct some research themselves to see which strategy works best for revision. They select two strategies and give each student two pieces of work to learn. The students are instructed to use Strategy 1 to learn the first piece of work and Strategy 2 for the second piece of work.
   a   Identify the experimental design used in this study.   (*1 mark*)
   b   Give **one** limitation with using this design in this study.   (*2 marks*)
   c   Explain how you might overcome this limitation.   (*3 marks*)

Continued on next page

Introduction   >   About this book
                           The AS exam
                           AS exam questions
                           How your answers are marked
                           AS exam advice
                           A mock exam

SECTION B: DEVELOPMENTAL PSYCHOLOGY AND RESEARCH METHODS

Answer **all** questions.

6 a Identify **one** cultural variation in attachment.   *(1 mark)*
   b Explain why this variation might occur in different cultures.   *(3 marks)*

7 Bowlby developed a theory of attachment.
   a Briefly outline the key elements of Bowlby's theory of attachment.   *(3 marks)*
   b Outline **one** study that has been used as support for Bowlby's theory of attachment.   *(4 marks)*

8 A number of studies have found that children who attend day care for more than 30 hours per week are more aggressive when they arrive at school. Dr Patel has decided to compare results found in America with day care centres in urban areas of India. For this study two items of data were collected for each child:
   • The number of hours they spent on average in day care per week. (Children who did not attend day care were excluded from the study.)
   • A score for aggressiveness based on teachers' rating of each child.
   a Identify the co-variables in this study.   *(2 marks)*
   b This study is looking at a correlation between two variables. Explain why you might expect to find a positive correlation between the variables.   *(2 marks)*
   c Explain **one** limitation of a study using a correlational analysis.   *(2 marks)*
   d Identify **one** ethical issue that might arise in this study and explain how you would deal with it. *(4 marks)*

9 David is doing his work experience at a day nursery. At the end of each day he notices that some of the children greet their parents enthusiastically whereas other children seem quite shy and sometimes even ignore their parents.
   Using your knowledge of attachment types, explain why such differences may occur.   *(3 marks)*

10 Outline and evaluate research into the effects of institutional care.   *(12 marks)*

PSYA 2 Mock exam

Time allowed: 1 hour and 30 minutes.
The marks for questions are shown in brackets.
Question 3 should be answered in continuous prose.

SECTION A: BIOLOGICAL PSYCHOLOGY

Answer **all** questions.

1 Type A individuals are more likely to experience negative effects from stressful experiences.
   a Explain what is meant by Type A and Type B behaviour.   *(3 marks)*
   b Using your knowledge of the body's response to stress, explain how stress may have negative effects. *(5 marks)*

2 Some psychologists have suggested that daily hassles are an important source of stress.
   How have psychologists investigated the relationship between daily hassles and stress?   *(4 marks)*

3 'Some people are more adversely affected by stress than others'.
   Outline and evaluate the role of personality factors in stress.   *(12 marks)*

Continued on next page

Introduction   > About this book
                                                  The AS exam
                                                  AS exam questions
                                                  How your answers are marked
                                                  AS exam advice
                                                  A mock exam

SECTION B: SOCIAL PSYCHOLOGY

Answer **all** questions.

4   Kayla and Jasmine are close friends and go to the same school. One of their teachers arranged for a
    speaker to come to the school to talk to the students about animal rights. After the talk, the speaker
    offered the students a chance to join his organisation and virtually everyone wanted to join, including
    Kayla and Jasmine. A few weeks later, Jasmine confided that she just joined because everyone else
    had. This surprised Kayla because she felt really committed to the cause and had volunteered to help
    out at a fundraising event.

    a   With reference to the example above, explain the concepts of 'internalisation' and 'compliance'.
                                                                                (3 marks + 3 marks)
    b   Outline how **one** research study has investigated the effects of conformity.   *(4 marks)*

5   Milgram's research into obedience has been criticised in terms of lacking validity.
    Describe and evaluate the validity of Milgram's research on obedience.   *(8 marks)*

6   A lot of research into social influence suggests that people are highly conformist and obedient. But
    research also shows that people can be independent in their behaviour.

    a   Outline **one** explanation of how people resist pressures to conform.   *(3 marks)*
    b   Outline **one** explanation of how people resist pressures to obey authority.   *(3 marks)*

SECTION C: INDIVIDUAL DIFFERENCES

Answer **all** questions.

7   The following statements are related to definitions of abnormality. Write down the letters that represent
    the **three** statements related to the 'deviation from social norms' definition.

A	Deviance is related to context and degree.
B	Abnormality is judged in terms of not being able to cope.
C	Abnormality is shown by a deviance from social standards.
D	The definition is open to abuse because norms vary across time and situation.
E	Mastery of the environment is an important criteria.

                                                                                           (3 marks)

8   Describe the key features of the psychodynamic model of abnormality.   *(4 marks)*

9   Daniel has been having difficulty sleeping since he lost his job. He has also lost all enthusiasm for life
    and can't motivate himself to do anything. He went to see his doctor about his problems and discussed
    various options including biological and psychological therapies.

    a   Daniel's doctor thought psychological therapies might be a better option. Outline **one** argument the
        doctor might use to convince Daniel that psychological therapies are better than biological ones.   *(3 marks)*
    b   The doctor thinks that Cognitive Behavioural Therapy might be the best psychological therapy.
        Outline what is involved in Cognitive Behavioural Therapy.   *(4 marks)*
    c   Daniel asks whether there are any drawbacks to using Cognitive Behavioural Therapy. What would
        you tell him?   *(3 marks)*

10 Psychologists conduct research to assess the effectiveness of any method used to treat abnormality.

    a   Describe how psychologists have investigated the effectiveness of drugs in treating abnormality.   *(3 marks)*
    b   Describe ethical issues that may arise when conducting research on the use of drugs to treat
        abnormality.   *(4 marks)*

Chapter 1

Cognitive psychology

Column 1: tick when you have produced brief notes.

Column 2: tick when you have a good grasp of this topic.

Column 3: tick during the final revision when you feel you have complete mastery of the topic.

Key terms • 3 marks' worth of material	1	2	3
Short-term memory (STM)	✔		
Long-term memory (LTM)	✔		
Encoding	✔		
Duration	✔		
Capacity	✔		
Eyewitness testimony (EWT)			
Misleading information			
Research studies related to … • **6 marks' worth of description** • **6 marks' worth of evaluation (including the issues of reliability, validity and ethics)**			
STM			
LTM			
Capacity			
Duration			
Encoding			
Multi-store model			
Working memory model			
Accuracy of EWT			
Effect of age of witness on EWT			
Effect of anxiety on EWT			
Effect of misleading questions in EWT			
Cognitive interview			
Strategies for memory improvement			
Factors that affect … • **6 marks' worth of material**			
Capacity of STM			
Duration of STM			
Encoding in STM and LTM			
Accuracy of EWT			
Explanations/theories • **6 marks' worth of description** • **6 marks' worth of evaluation (both strengths and limitations)**			
Multi-store model			
Working memory model			
Applications of memory research • **6 marks' worth of material**			
Strategies for memory improvement			

Cognitive psychology: Memory	>	Models of memory	>	Nature of memory
Developmental psychology: Attachment		Memory in everyday life	>	Multi-store model of memory
Research methods				Working memory model
Biological psychology: Stress				
Social psychology: Social influence				
Individual differences: Psychopathology (abnormality)				

KEY TERMS

Capacity
- A measure of how much can be held in memory.
- Measured in terms of bits of information, such as number of digits.

Duration
- A measure of how long a memory lasts before it is no longer available.

Encoding
- The way information is changed so it can be stored in memory.
- Information enters the brain via the senses (e.g. eyes and ears) and is then stored in various forms, such as visual codes (like a picture), acoustic forms (sounds), or a semantic form (the meaning of the experience).

Long-term memory (LTM)
- Memory for events that have happened in the past.
- Lasts anywhere from 2 minutes to 100 years.
- Potentially unlimited duration and capacity.

Short-term memory (STM)
- Memory for immediate events.
- Lasts for a very short time and disappears unless it is rehearsed.
- Limited duration and limited capacity.
- Sometimes referred to as *working memory*.

	STM	LTM
Duration	Measured in seconds and minutes	Measured in hours, days and years
Capacity	Less than 7 chunks	Potentially unlimited
Encoding	Acoustic (i.e. information represented as sounds) or visual	Semantic (i.e. information represented by its meaning)

Duration of STM

keySTUDY Peterson and Peterson (1959)

How? Lab experiment. Participants: 24 students. Participants were given a *consonant syllable* (e.g. WRT) to be remembered and also given a three-digit number. They were asked to count backwards from the number until told to stop and recall the **nonsense trigram**. This was repeated eight times with different retention intervals: 3, 6, 9, 12, 15 or 18 seconds.

Showed? Participants could remember about 90% of the consonant syllables when there was only a 3 second interval, which dropped to about 20% after 9 seconds and about 2% when there was an 18 second interval. This suggests that STM has a duration of less than 18 seconds if verbal rehearsal is prevented. In fact, much of the information has disappeared within a few seconds.

Evaluation

Validity (1) **Ecological validity**: the stimulus material is artificial and therefore findings may not apply to all aspects of everyday life, though it does apply to memorising verbal material. (2) **Internal validity**: were they testing duration? Trigrams may have been displaced by numbers when counting backwards and therefore forgetting was not due to spontaneous **decay** but, instead, due to **displacement**.

Duration of STM may be shorter – Marsh *et al.* suggested that Peterson and Peterson's high levels of recall were because participants knew they would be tested on recall. When Marsh *et al.* conducted a similar study and tested participants without warning, forgetting occurred after just 2 seconds.

Duration of STM may be longer – Nairne *et al.* asked participants to recall the *same* items across trials, whereas in the earlier study different items were used on each trial, which would have led to interference between items, decreasing recall. In Nairne *et al.*'s study duration of STM was as long as 96 seconds. Therefore it seems that information remains for quite a while in STM *unless* other material replaces or overwrites it.

Duration of LTM

Research evidence

Shepard conducted a **lab experiment** to test the duration of LTM. He showed participants 612 memorable pictures, one at a time. An hour later they were shown some of these pictures within a set of others and displayed almost perfect recognition. Four months later they were still able to recognise 50% of the photographs.

Bahrick *et al.* conducted a **natural experiment**. They asked people of various ages to put names to faces from their high school year book and 48 years on, people were about 70% accurate. In this case, the material to be remembered was more meaningful to the participants and therefore the duration of the long-term memories was better.

Evaluation

Generalisability – It is difficult to find tasks that can truly represent long-term memories. In Shepherd's study (above) participants would not have much interest in the pictures, which would have affected the duration of the memories. In Bahrick *et al.*'s study (above) participants may have seen some of their classmates over the years which would explain high levels of recall.

Cognitive psychology: Memory	>	Models of memory	>	Nature of memory
Developmental psychology: Attachment	>	Memory in everyday life	>	Multi-store model of memory
Research methods	>			Working memory model
Biological psychology: Stress	>			
Social psychology: Social influence	>			
Individual differences: Psychopathology (abnormality)	>			

KEY TERMS

Chunking

- Miller proposed that the capacity of STM can be enhanced by grouping sets of digits or letters into meaningful units or 'chunks'.
- For example it is easier to remember 100 1000 10 10000 than 10010001010000.
- Miller suggested we can remember 7 ± 2 chunks at a time.
- The size of a chunk may affect how many other chunks can be processed.

Digit span technique

- A technique to assess the span of immediate (short-term) memory.
- Participants are given progressively more digits in a list to see how many can be recalled.

Capacity of STM

Research evidence

Miller reviewed previous research and concluded that the span of **STM** is 7 ± 2, e.g. people can cope reasonably well with counting 7 dots flashed onto a screen but not many more than this.

Jacobs used the **digit span technique** to assess the capacity of STM. He found the average span for digits was 9.3 items, whereas it was 7.3 for letters. It may be easier to recall digits because there are only 10 possible digits (0–9) wheras there are 26 letters.

Chunking – Miller also found that people can recall 5 *words* as well as they can recall 5 *letters* – we **chunk** things together and then can remember more. **Simon** conducted a **lab experiment**. He found that the size of the chunk matters – people had a shorter span for larger chunks, such as 8-word phrases, than smaller chunks, such as one-syllable words.

Evaluation

- **Capacity of STM may be more limited – Cowan** reviewed a variety of studies on the capacity of STM and concluded that STM is likely to be limited to about 4 chunks.
- **Individual differences – Jacobs** also found that digit span increased with age; 8-year-olds could remember an average of 6.6 digits, whereas the mean for 19-year-olds was 8.6 digits. This might be due to a gradual increase in brain capacity, and/or that people develop strategies to improve their digit span, such as **chunking**.
- **Real-world application – Baddeley** discovered that if the initial letters of a postcode were meaningful (e.g. BS for Bristol) it made the postcode easier to remember. Numbers were best remembered if they were placed between the city name and random letters.

Encoding in STM and LTM

keySTUDY Baddeley (1966)

How? Lab experiment. Participants were given lists of words that were acoustically similar (sounded the same) or dissimilar and words that were semantically similar (meant the same) or dissimilar.

Showed? Participants had more difficulty remembering acoustically similar words in STM but not in LTM, whereas semantically similar words posed little problem for short-term recall but led to muddled long-term memories.

Evaluation

- **Brandimote et al.** conducted a **lab experiment**. They found that participants used visual encoding in STM if they were given a *visual* task (pictures) and were prevented from doing any *verbal* rehearsal in the retention interval (they had to say 'la la la' before performing a *visual* recall task). Normally we 'translate' visual images into verbal codes in STM, but since verbal rehearsal was prevented, they used visual codes.

Wickens et al. found that STM sometimes uses a semantic code rather than being restricted to acoustic coding.

In LTM **Frost** showed that recall was related to visual as well as semantic categories. **Nelson and Rothbart** found evidence of acoustic coding in LTM.

⟳ PUTTING IT ALL TOGETHER

Research supports a distinction between STM and LTM in terms of duration (less than 18 seconds or forever), capacity (less than 7 chunks or infinite) and encoding (*generally* acoustic or semantic).

15

Cognitive psychology: Memory	>	Models of memory	>	Nature of memory
Developmental psychology: Attachment		Memory in everyday life	>	Multi-store model of memory
Research methods	>			Working memory model
Biological psychology: Stress	>			
Social psychology: Social influence	>			
Individual differences: Psychopathology (abnormality)	>			

KEY TERMS

Multi-store model (MSM)
- An explanation of memory.
- Based on three separate memory stores and how information is transferred between these stores.

Sensory memory (SM)
- Information at the senses – information collected by your eyes, ears, nose, fingers and so on.
- Information is retained for a very brief period by the sensory registers (less than half a second).
- Capacity of sensory memory is very large.
- Method of encoding depends on the sense organ involved, i.e. visual for the eyes, acoustic for the ears.

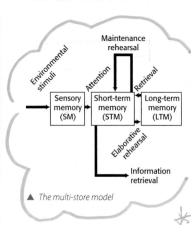

▲ The multi-store model

PUTTING IT ALL TOGETHER

Research supports the view that there are a number of different memory stores which are quantitatively and qualitatively different, as described by the multi-store model. However the multi-store model is oversimplified.

Multi-store model (Atkinson and Shiffrin, 1968)

- An explanation of how memory processes work based on the idea that there are three separate stores (**SM, STM, LTM**).
- Each store has unique characteristics: **duration, capacity** and **encoding**.
- Information first arrives at SM. Attention causes transference to STM.
- Information in STM is in a fragile state, and disappears if not rehearsed (**decay**) or if new information enters (**displacement**).
- Increasing rehearsal leads to transfer from STM to LTM; the more rehearsal of an item the better it is remembered.
- Rehearsal is maintenance rehearsal (verbal) but also elaborative rehearsal.

Research evidence supporting the MSM

Sensory memory – Sperling conducted a **lab experiment**. He asked participants to report 12 letters/digits from a three line display after a 50 millisecond delay. Recall was poorer for all items (5 items recalled, about 42%) than when asked to give one row only (3 items recalled, 75%). This shows that information decays rapidly in the sensory store.

Serial position effect – Glanzer and Cunitz conducted a lab experiment. They gave participants a list of words and found that words recalled tended to be from the start of the list (**primacy effect**) and end of list (**recency effect**). This **serial position effect** occurs because the first words are best rehearsed and transferred to LTM, and the last words are in STM when you start recalling the list.

Brain scans – Beardsley used **brain scanning** to investigate brain activity and found that the **prefrontal cortex** is active during STM tasks. **Squire et al.** also used brain scanning and found the **hippocampus** is active when LTM is engaged. This shows there are distinct stores.

Case study of HM – Scoville and Milner conducted a **case study**. They found that the ability to form new LTM was impaired when the hippocampus was removed; LTMs formed prior to the operation remained intact.

Evaluation

Strengths

Research support e.g. studies above and on previous pages related to duration, capacity, encoding.

Produces testable predictions, which is important for the scientific process to enable theory testing and verification.

Limitations

STM and LTM are not unitary stores. STM has verbal and visual stores (see WMM on facing page) and LTM is divided into semantic, episodic and procedural memory as well as perceptual-representation system (PRS). Supported by **Spiers et al.** who studied amnesiac patients, whose procedural and PRS systems were intact but not the other types of LTM.

Rehearsal involves processing (elaboration) as well as maintenance. Supported by **Craik and Tulving** who found that words processed more deeply (semantically) were better remembered.

STM not entirely separate from LTM. **Ruchkin et al.** found participants' brain activity was different when they processed real or pseudo-words.

Cognitive psychology: Memory	>	Models of memory	>	Nature of memory
Developmental psychology: Attachment	>	Memory in everyday life	>	Multi-store model of memory
Research methods	>			Working memory model
Biological psychology: Stress	>			
Social psychology: Social influence	>			
Individual differences: Psychopathology (abnormality)	>			

KEY TERMS

Central executive
- Monitors and coordinates all other mental functions in WM.

Episodic buffer
- Receives input from many sources.
- Temporarily stores this information.
- Integrates it in order to construct a mental episode of what is being experienced right now.

Phonological loop
- Encodes speech sounds.
- Involves maintenance rehearsal (repeating the words over and over again, i.e. a *loop*).
- Divided into **phonological store** (inner ear) and **articulatory process** (inner voice).

Visuo-spatial sketchpad
- Encodes visual information.
- Divided into the **visual cache** (stores information) and **inner scribe** (spatial relations).

Word-length effect
- People remember lists of short words better than long words.
- Governed by the capacity of the phonological loop.

Working memory model (WMM)
- An explanation of STM, called 'working memory'.
- Based on four components, some with storage capacity.

Working memory model (Baddeley and Hitch, 1974)

- An explanation of STM (i.e. the memory used when working on something, such as solving problems, comprehending language, etc.).
- **Central executive** is an attentional process to monitor incoming data and allocate 'slave systems' to tasks. Has very limited capacity.
- **Phonological loop** deals with auditory information and preserves its order. Subdivided into **phonological store**, which stores the words you hear, and **articulatory process**, which allows maintenance rehearsal – repeating the words.
- **Visuo-spatial sketchpad** stores visual and/or spatial information. Subdivided into **visual cache**, which stores visual data, and **inner scribe**, which encodes the arrangement of objects in the visual field.
- **Episodic buffer** provides a temporary store and links with LTM.

Research evidence supporting the WMM

Dual task performance – Hitch and Baddeley conducted a **lab experiment**. They demonstrated that performance was slower when participants were given a task involving the central executive and a second task involving both the central executive and the articulatory loop, than the articulatory loop alone or no extra task.

Evidence for the four components:
Central executive – Bunge *et al*. used **fMRI** to demonstrate greater activation in certain parts of the brain when participants engaged in dual-task activity rather than single task, reflecting increased attentional demands.

Phonological loop – Baddeley *et al*. conducted a lab experiment. They demonstrated that the phonological loop holds the amount of information that can be said in 2 seconds. However, the **word-length effect** disappears if a person is given an **articulatory suppression task** (a repetitive task that ties up the articulatory process).

Visuo-spatial sketchpad – Baddeley *et al*. conducted a lab experiment. They showed that participants had more difficulty doing two visual tasks (track light and describing what the letter F looks like) than a visual and verbal task, evidence of visuo-spatial sketchpad.

Evidence from case studies – Shallice and Warrington conducted a **case study** of KF whose LTM was intact, as was STM for visual stimuli, but he had poor STM ability with verbal material (letters and digits but not sounds).

Evaluation

Strengths
Explanatory power – The WMM can explain a number of research findings that can't be explained by the MSM, e.g. the word-length effect and partial memory difficulties experienced by patients such as KF.

Comparison with MSM – The MSM was a first step in understanding the components of memory. The WMM expands the MSM by further defining separate stores, offering a better account of STM because it distinguishes between different stores and processes within STM.

Limitations
Central executive is vaguely defined and doesn't really explain anything. May consist of separate components.

Evidence from brain-damaged patients may not be informative because you cannot make 'before and after' comparisons, so it is not clear whether changes in behaviour are caused by the damage. Also the process of brain injury is traumatic, which may in itself change behaviour.

PUTTING IT ALL TOGETHER

The working memory model offers a refinement of the multi-store model, describing working memory in terms of specialised auditory and visual units.

17

Cognitive psychology: Memory	>	Models of memory	>	Eyewitness testimony
Developmental psychology: Attachment		Memory in everyday life	>	Cognitive interview
Research methods				Strategies for memory improvement
Biological psychology: Stress	>			
Social psychology: Social influence	>			
Individual differences: Psychopathology (abnormality)	>			

The effect of misleading information on EWT

keySTUDY Loftus and Palmer (1974)

Experiment 1

How? **Lab experiment**. Forty-five students were shown films of traffic accidents. Questions afterwards included a critical one about speed of car. These questions used the verb 'hit', 'smashed', 'collided', 'bumped' or 'contacted'.

Showed? The group who heard the verb 'smashed' estimated a higher speed, the group who heard the word 'contacted' estimated the lowest speed (see graph on right). Suggests that leading questions (**post-event information**) can have a significant effect on memory (could be on how memory is stored or how it is retrieved).

Experiment 2 to investigate whether post-event information alters storage or retrieval.

How? A different set of participants were shown a film of an accident. A week later they were asked whether there was any broken glass.

Showed? Those who heard the question with 'smashed' were more likely to recollect broken glass (there was none) (see graph on right). Shows that post-event information affects initial storage.

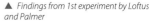
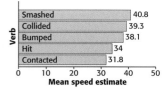

▲ *Findings from 1st experiment by Loftus and Palmer*

Evaluation

Loftus *et al.* supported the original findings with a further lab experiment. Participants were shown photos of a car at a junction with STOP or YIELD sign. They were then given questions that were either consistent with the photo seen (e.g. participant saw photo of a STOP sign and asked about a car at a STOP sign) or inconsistent (e.g. participants saw photo of a YIELD sign but asked about a car at a STOP sign). Finally they were shown pairs of photos and ask to identify which was the original photo. Those given inconsistent (i.e. misleading) information were 41% correct in their identification compared to 75% correct when consistent questions were used. Shows that misleading information affects recall.

Bekerian and Bowers conducted a lab experiment. They investigated whether misleading information alters the way information is stored or how it is retrieved, repeating the STOP/YIELD study. When participants were given a question that matched the sign they had been shown (stop or yield) their recall was more accurate when questions were consistent than inconsistent. But when the slides were presented in the right sequence, misleading information (inconsistent question) had no effect. This suggests that misleading information affects retrieval rather than storage.

Validity – Research findings may lack validity because the experimental setting is not true to life. Participants may not take the experimental task seriously and thus behaviour does not represent real EWT. **Foster** *et al.* showed that recall is more accurate in real life.

Real-world application – Wells and Olsen reported that mistaken eyewitness identification was the largest single factor in convicting innocent people. Psychological research has been crucial in providing a scientific understanding of how misleading information may affect EWT.

Individual differences (1) **Gender** – men and women take an interest in different aspects of a scene but both are equally accurate (**Wells and Olsen**). (2) **Age** – elderly people are less able to remember the source of information than are younger people (misinformation effect) (**Schacter** *et al.*).

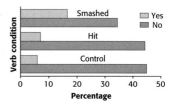
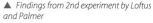

▲ *Findings from 2nd experiment by Loftus and Palmer*

KEY TERMS

Eyewitness testimony (EWT)

- The evidence provided in court by a person who witnessed a crime, with a view to identifying the perpetrator of the crime.

- The accuracy of eyewitness recall may be affected during initial encoding, subsequent storage and eventual retrieval.

Misleading information

- Information that, either by its form or content, suggests to the witness what answer is desired, or leads him to the desired answer.

Cognitive psychology: Memory	>	Models of memory	>	Eyewitness testimony
Developmental psychology: Attachment		Memory in everyday life	>	Cognitive interview
Research methods				Strategies for memory improvement
Biological psychology: Stress				
Social psychology: Social influence				
Individual differences: Psychopathology (abnormality)				

KEY TERMS

Anxiety

- A nervous emotional state where we fear that something unpleasant is about to happen.
- People often become anxious in stressful situations.
- Anxiety tends to be accompanied by physiological arousal (e.g. a pounding heart and rapid shallow breathing). Therefore research in this area is often focused on the effects of arousal.

The effect of anxiety on EWT

Research evidence

Anxiety has a negative effect – Deffenbacher et al. conducted a **meta-analysis**. They analysed 18 studies of anxiety and EWT. Many showed that stress has a negative impact on accuracy of EWT but some studies showed that anxiety may actually enhance the accuracy of recall.

Anxiety enhances recall – Christianson and Hubinette conducted a **questionnaire**. They spoke to 58 real witnesses to bank robberies. The greater the threat, the more accurate the recall and the more detail was remembered, compared to onlookers who were less emotionally aroused.

The weapon–focus effect – Johnson and Scott conducted a **lab experiment** to demonstrate the **weapon focus effect** – arousal (anxiety) may focus attention on central features of a crime (e.g. the weapon) and thus reduce recall of details (e.g. of perpetrator's face). In this experiment, a man runs through a room carrying a pen covered in grease or knife covered in blood. Witnesses were 49% accurate in identifying the man with the pen, compared to 33% accuracy with the knife.

Evaluation

Contradictory findings can be explained in terms of the **Yerkes-Dodson law** – medium levels of arousal (anxiety) enhance accurate recall, whereas high levels decrease it.

Research supports weapon-focus effect, e.g. a meta-analysis by **Steblay** showed support. Also **Loftus et al.** tracked eyewitnesses' eye movements showing they were looking at a weapon rather than a potential criminal's face.

Real-world application – Rinolo et al. used evidence from the sinking of the Titanic, where 75% of the survivors had reported that the ship broke apart when sinking. Their testimony was regarded as inaccurate until the wreck was discovered and their account was proved right. This supports the view that anxiety does not necessarily result in inaccurate recall.

The effect of age on EWT

Research evidence

The following studies are all **natural or quasi-experiments** because the IV (age) varies naturally.

Children as witnesses – Parker and Carranza found that primary school children were more likely to choose someone from a mock line-up than were adults, but they were also more likely to make errors.

Age differences in accuracy – Yarmey found that older adults (age 45–65) were less confident in recall of a confederate but not less accurate than younger adults.

Effects of delay – Memon et al. found that accuracy in older people (age 60–82) dropped when the identification task was delayed for a week.

Evaluation

Own-age bias – Apparent superior performance of younger people may be because the faces to be recognised are younger faces. **Anastasi and Rhodes** found that all age groups are most accurate when the target photographs are from their own age group.

Explaining own-age bias – The less contact we have with certain groups of people, the poorer our ability to discriminate between individuals in this group (= **differential experience hypothesis, Brigham and Malpas**).

Individual differences – Clifasefi et al. showed that mildly intoxicated participants were less observant than sober participants; 82% of the intoxicated group failed to notice a man in a gorilla costume who walked across a room during a video of people playing basketball whereas only 46% of sober participants didn't notice.

Research methods – Participants may not behave as they would in everyday life in studies that are conducted in a 'lab'. They may not take the task as seriously as in real life or they may be looking for cues, something they wouldn't do in everyday life.

PUTTING IT ALL TOGETHER

Eyewitness testimony may lack accuracy in some situations, e.g. because of misleading questions, high arousal or identifying people of a different age group. However it may also be impressively accurate.

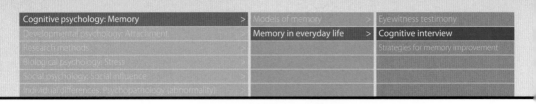

Cognitive psychology: Memory	>	Models of memory	>	Eyewitness testimony
Developmental psychology: Attachment	>	Memory in everyday life	>	Cognitive interview
Research methods	>			Strategies for memory improvement
Biological psychology: Stress	>			
Social psychology: Social influence	>			
Individual differences: Psychopathology (abnormality)	>			

KEY TERMS

Cognitive interview (CI)

- A police technique for interviewing witnesses to a crime.
- Based on what psychologists have found out about memory.
- Because our memory is made up of a network of associations rather than of discrete events, memories are best accessed using multiple retrieval strategies.
- Unlike a standard interview, the CI encourages witnesses to recreate the original context so as to increase the accessibility of stored information.

Standard interview

- An interview that lacks the four CI components.

The cognitive interview (Fisher and Gieselman, 1992)

1 **Report everything** – Include every single detail of the event, even though it may seem irrelevant. Aims to increase consistency between actual event and the recreated situation, leading to increased likeliness that witnesses will recall more details, and be more accurate in their recall.

2 **Mental reinstatement of original context** – Mentally recreate the environment from the original incident. Aim is same as for no.1.

3 **Changing the order** – e.g. reversing the order in which events occurred. Aims to vary route through memory in order to increase recall and to remove the effects of 'scripts' (a person's memory for routine activities – once a 'script' is triggered elements of a scene are filled in without thinking).

4 **Changing the perspective** – Recall the incident from multiple perspectives, e.g. imagining how it would have appeared to other witnesses present at the time. Aim is same as for no.3.

Enhanced CI includes additional techniques for probing witnesses' mental image of an event.

⬡ Evaluation

Research into the effectiveness of CI – Köhnken *et al. conducted a **meta-analysis** of 53 studies and found a 34% increase in correct recall using CI compared with **standard interview**. **Milne and Bull** conducted a **lab experiment** using college students and children, and found that steps 1 and 2 (report everything and mental reinstatement) gave better recall than using just one component. They also found that using just one component was no better than an instruction to 'try again'.

Difficulties in establishing effectiveness – There are many versions of CI used by different police forces, which makes comparison difficult. Thames Valley use the whole procedure whereas others just use one or two components (**Kebbell and Wagstaff**).

Time problems with CI – As the CI is more time-consuming than the standard interview, police officers prefer to use strategies that limit the amount of information collected (**Kebbell and Wagstaff**).

Enhanced CI – Fisher and Geiselman added further cognitive techniques for probing a witness's mental image of an event. This creates additional problems because it places even greater demands on the interviewer.

Individual differences – The CI may be particular effective with older witnesses who are overcautious about reporting what they saw. **Mello and Fisher** found greater improvements using the CI with older rather than younger participants, but there were no differences when using the standard interview.

Real-world application – Stein and Memon tested female cleaning staff in Brazil and found increased recall, especially for details that would be useful, e.g. description of man holding the gun.

⟳ PUTTING IT ALL TOGETHER

The cognitive interview is based on psychological insights into memory processes and has proved effective, though the limitations (e.g. too time-consuming) may outweigh the advantages.

Cognitive psychology: Memory	>	Models of memory	>	Eyewitness testimony
Developmental psychology: Attachment		Memory in everyday life	>	Cognitive interview
Research methods				Strategies for memory improvement
Biological psychology: Stress				
Social psychology: Social influence				
Individual differences: Psychopathology (abnormality)				

Memory improvement

Verbal techniques

1 **Acronyms** – e.g. ROYGBIV to remember the colours of the rainbow: **R**ed, **O**range, **Y**ellow, **G**reen, **B**lue, **I**ndigo, **V**iolet.

2 **Acrostics** – e.g. **M**y **V**ery **E**asy **M**ethod **J**ust **S**peeds **U**p **N**aming **P**lanets is used to remember the order of the planets: **M**ercury, **V**enus, **E**arth, **M**ars, **J**upiter, **S**aturn, **U**ranus, **N**eptune, **P**luto.

3 **Rhymes** – e.g. using the tune of *Twinkle Twinkle Little Star* to remember the letters of the alphabet.

4 **Chunking** – e.g. telephone numbers and post codes.

Evaluation

Research evidence – Gruneberg found 30% of psychology students revised using mnemonics, especially acronyms and acrostics. **Glidden et al.** found verbal mnemonics were effective in children with learning disabilities, although not in the long term.

Real-world applications – Broadly and MacDonald studied 63 children with Down syndrome. An experimental group received training in memory improvement techniques (rehearsal and organisation) and showed improved short-term memory skills in comparison to a control group.

Role of organisation – Bower et al. conducted a **lab experiment**. They gave participants 112 words to learn. Recall was 2–3 times better if the words were presented in an organised hierarchy rather than in a random order. Our memories naturally organise themselves, making links – using mnemonic techniques merely speeds up this process.

Limitations of mnemonic strategies – Research is often conducted in lab conditions with materials appropriate to mnemonic strategies, therefore may not apply to everyday life. **Slavin** did not find that memory techniques work in 'real' contexts, e.g. in speaking foreign languages better.

PUTTING IT ALL TOGETHER

Research shows that people who learn about **mnemonic techniques** are better at learning material, so these techniques work. However it is important to select the appropriate technique for the task.

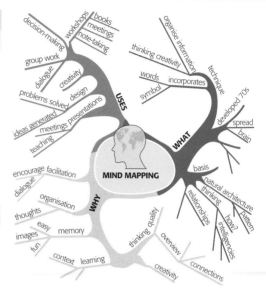

▲ *A mind map about mind mapping*

Visual techniques

1 **Method of loci** – Learner associates material to be learned with different locations in a house, along a road, etc. Then the learner mentally retraces their steps to recall the items.

2 **Keyword method** – Used when associating pieces of information, e.g. learning a new language. The new word is broken into components with images created for each component that link to English meaning.

3 **Mind maps** – Main topic is placed in the centre and then branching links are made producing a unique visual appearance.

Evaluation

Research evidence – O'Hara et al. found that training in the use of mnemonic techniques (e.g. method of loci) has long-term memory benefits for older adults. **Atkinson** found that participants using keywords learned significantly more Russian vocabulary than a control group not using the method. However, the long-term advantage of the keyword technique is less well supported.

Role of elaborative rehearsal – Craik and Tulving's research (see page 16) showed that elaboration (e.g. creating a mind map or using the method of loci) leads to more enduring memories.

Dual coding hypothesis – Pavio suggested that words and images are processed separately (based on the fact that some brain damaged individuals can process one but not the other). Therefore, concrete words will be remembered better because they are double-encoded – once as a word, and once as a visual image.

Chapter 2

Developmental psychology

Column 1: tick when you have produced brief notes.

Column 2: tick when you have a good grasp of this topic.

Column 3: tick during the final revision when you feel you have complete mastery of the topic.

Key terms • **3 marks' worth of material**	1	2	3
Attachment			
Secure attachment			
Insecure-avoidant attachment			
Insecure-resistant attachment			
Disruption of attachment			
Failure to form attachment (privation)			
Institutional care			
Day care			
Research studies related to … • **6 marks' worth of description** • **6 marks' worth of evaluation (including the issues of reliability, validity and ethics)**			
Learning theory explanation of attachment			
Bowlby's theory of attachment			
Types of attachment			
Cultural variations in attachment			
Disruption of attachment			
Failure to form attachment (privation)			
Effects of institutional care			
Impact of day care on social development			
Impact of day care on aggression			
Impact of day care on peer relations			
Factors that affect … • **6 marks' worth of material**			
Types of attachment			
Effects of disruption of attachment			
Effects of failure to form attachment (privation)			
Effects of institutional care			
Impact of day care on social development			
Impact of day care on aggression			
Impact of day care on peer relations			
Explanations/theories • **6 marks' worth of description** • **6 marks' worth of evaluation (both strengths and limitations)**			
Learning theory			
Bowlby's theory (evolutionary perspective)			
Applications of attachment research • **6 marks' worth of material**			
Influence of attachment research			
Influence of day care research			

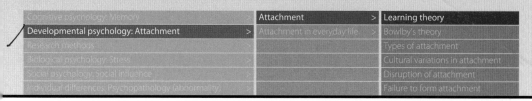

	Attachment >	Learning theory
Cognitive psychology: Memory		Bowlby's theory
Developmental psychology: Attachment >	Attachment in everyday life >	
Research methods >		Types of attachment
Biological psychology: Stress >		Cultural variations in attachment
Social psychology: Social influence >		Disruption of attachment
Individual differences: Psychopathology (abnormality) >		Failure to form attachment

KEY TERMS

Attachment
- An emotional bond between two people.
- A two-way process that endures over time.
- Leads to certain behaviours such as clinging and proximity-seeking.
- Serves the function of protecting an infant.

Classical conditioning
- A new response (**conditioned response**, **CR**) is learned when a **neutral stimulus** (**NS**) is associated with an **unconditioned stimulus** (**UCS**). Initially, the UCS produced an **unconditioned response** (**UCR**). After learning, the NS becomes a **conditioned stimulus** (**CS**) which produces a CR.
- 'Unconditioned' means learning was not required.

Learning theory
- The name given to a group of explanations, i.e. classical and operant conditioning.
- Essentially, these explain behaviour in terms of learning rather than any inborn tendencies (the biological/ evolutionary approach) or higher order thinking (the cognitive approach).

Operant conditioning
- Each time you do something and it results in a *pleasant consequence*, the behaviour is 'stamped in' (**reinforcement**). It becomes more probable that you will repeat that behaviour in the future.
- If you do something and it results in an *unpleasant consequence* (**punishment**), it becomes less likely that you will repeat that behaviour.
- A **reinforcer** is any that is experienced as rewarding. A **primary reinforcer** is an innate reinforcer. A **secondary reinforcer** is one that is acquired through experience.

Explanations of attachment: Learning theory

⬡ Explanation

Classical conditioning – learning through association
- *Before conditioning*
  Food (**UCS**) produces a sense of pleasure (**UCR**).
- *During conditioning*
  Food (**UCS**) and the presence of a person who feeds the infant (**NS**) occur together a number of times. The NS gradually becomes a conditioned stimulus (**CS**).
- *After conditioning*
  Person who feeds the infant (**CS**) produces pleasure (now a **CR**).

Operant conditioning – learning through reinforcement
- Dollard and Miller suggested that attachment is based on **reinforcement**.
- Hungry infant feels uncomfortable, creating a drive to reduce discomfort.
- When the infant is fed, the drive is reduced and this produces a feeling of pleasure (which is reinforcing). Food becomes a **primary reinforcer**.
- The person who supplies the food is associated with avoiding discomfort and becomes a **secondary reinforcer**, a source of reward.
- Attachment occurs because the infant seeks the person who can supply the reward.

⬡ Evaluation

Strength
Learning theory can explain attachment – Infants do acquire attachment through association and reinforcement but the reinforcer is not food. For example, a caregiver who is responsive to the babies needs is providing reinforcement and this encourages the attachment.

Limitations
Contact comfort is more important – People believe that feeding plays a key role in attachment but the evidence shows otherwise. **Harlow** conducted an **animal experiment** in a lab. Infant rhesus monkeys were placed in a cage with two wire mothers – the 'lactating mother' had a feeding bottle attached and the other was wrapped in soft cloth but offered no food. The monkeys spent most time with the cloth-covered mother and would cling to it especially when they were frightened (a proximity-seeking behaviour which is characteristic of attachment).

Human studies also challenge the importance of food in attachment – **Schaffer and Emerson** conducted a **controlled observation** of 60 babies in their own homes for a period of about a year. They found that infants were *not* most attached to the person who fed them. The strongest attachments were to the person who was most responsive and who interacted with them the most.

⊂ PUTTING IT ALL TOGETHER

'Cupboard love' is not likely to be the best explanation for attachment because research shows that infants do not necessarily become most strongly attached to the person who feeds them. However, classical and operant conditioning may be part of the story of attachment because attention and responsiveness can be reinforcing.

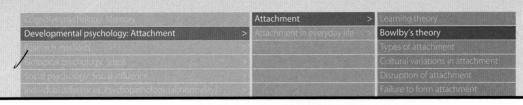

Cognitive psychology: Memory		Attachment	>	Learning theory
Developmental psychology: Attachment	>	Attachment in everyday life	>	Bowlby's theory
Research methods	>			Types of attachment
Biological psychology: Stress	>			Cultural variations in attachment
Social psychology: Social influence	>			Disruption of attachment
Individual differences: Psychopathology (abnormality)	>			Failure to form attachment

KEY TERMS

Continuity hypothesis
- The view that there is a link between an infant's early attachment relationship and later behaviour.

Internal working model
- A cluster of concepts about relationships.
- In the short term, it gives the child insight into the caregiver's behaviour.
- In the long term, it acts as a template for future relationships because it generates expectations about how people behave.

Monotropy
- The idea that the one relationship that the infant has with his/her primary attachment figure is of special significance in emotional development.

Primary attachment figure
- The person who has formed the closest bond with a child.
- Demonstrated by the intensity of the relationship.
- Usually a child's biological mother, but could be an adoptive mother, a father, grandmother, etc.

Secondary attachment figure
- Acts as a kind of emotional safety net.
- Contributes to social development.

Sensitive period
- A biologically-determined period of time during which a child is particularly sensitive to a specific form of stimulation, around 3–6 months of age.
- Resulting in the development of a specific response or characteristic.

Social releasers
- A social behaviour or characteristic which elicits a caregiving reaction.

Temperament hypothesis
- The view that attachment type can be explained in terms of an infant's innate temperament rather than caregiver sensitivity.

Explanations of attachment: Bowlby's theory (1969)

- Babies have an innate drive to become attached and also are born with certain characteristics, called **social releasers**, which elicit caregiving.
- Attachment develops during a **sensitive period**, around 3–6 months. Later, it becomes increasingly difficult to form attachments.
- Infants have one special emotional bond (**monotropy**) with their **primary attachment figure**.
- Infants have bonds with many **secondary attachment figures**. These are important for healthy psychological and social development.
- The mother–infant relationship creates expectations about relationships, leading to an **internal working model**.
- The **continuity hypothesis** is that individuals who are securely attached in infancy *continue* to be socially and emotionally competent.

⬡ Evaluation

Strengths
Evidence suggests that attachment is an innate process, as suggested by Bowlby – evidence about imprinting from studies of non-human animals (e.g. **Lorenz**) shows that bond formation between adult and infant is innate.

Furthermore **cross-cultural studies** show that similar patterns of attachment develop in all cultures, e.g. **Tronick et al.**'s cross-cultural study of the Efe from Zaire (infants are looked after and even breastfed by different women but still form one primary attachment). This suggests that attachment must be innate.

The concept of monotropy is supported by research. **Schaffer and Emerson**'s **controlled observation** found that infants formed many attachments but there was still one *primary* object of attachment, which most often (but not always) was the infant's mother.

The importance of secure attachment in emotional development (the continuity hypothesis) – **Harlow**'s **animal experiment** showed that monkeys raised with an unresponsive wire 'mother' (no secure attachments) developed into emotionally maladjusted adults. Also a **longitudinal study** by **Sroufe et al.** (Minnesota longitudinal study) found that those infants classified as secure were later rated highest for social competence and popularity. These studies show that early secure attachments are related to social adjustment later in life.

Limitations
Multiple attachments and monotropy. Not clear whether only one primary attachment is necessary for healthy emotional development; several may be desirable (**Rutter**).

Alternative explanation, the **temperament hypothesis** – **Kagan** suggested that attachment could be explained in terms of innate temperamental types. Infants who have an 'easy' temperament are more likely to become securely attached and those who are 'difficult' tend to be insecurely attached. Supported in research by **Belsky and Rovine** but not by **Nachmias et al.**

↻ PUTTING IT ALL TOGETHER

Bowlby's evolutionary approach to understanding attachment as an adaptive behaviour for both infant and parent continues to be the most preferred explanation for attachment behaviour.

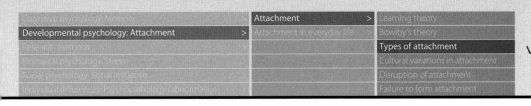

	Attachment	>	Learning theory
Developmental psychology: Attachment	>	Attachment in everyday life	>	Bowlby's theory
			Types of attachment
			Cultural variations in attachment
			Disruption of attachment
			Failure to form attachment

Cognitive psychology: Memory
Research methods
Biological psychology: Stress
Social psychology: Social influence
Individual differences: Psychopathology (abnormality)

KEY TERMS

Insecure attachment
- Develops as a result of caregiver's lack of sensitive responding to an infant's needs.
- May be associated with poor cognitive and emotional development.
- **Insecure-avoidant** infants are willing to explore and unresponsive to mother's return; they generally avoid social interaction and intimacy with others.
- **Insecure-resistant (ambivalent)** infants who are less interested in exploring and show distress on mother's return; generally they both seek and reject intimacy and social interaction.
- **Insecure-disorganised** infants who lack consistent patterns of attachment behaviour.
- **Disinhibited** infants who display affection to strangers and may be attention-seeking.

Secure attachment
- Willing to explore, easy to soothe, high stranger anxiety.
- Infant is comfortable with social interaction and intimacy.
- Related to healthy subsequent cognitive and emotional development.
- Develops as a result of sensitive responding by caregiver to the infant's needs.

Separation anxiety
- Distress shown by an infant when separated from his/her attachment figure.

Strange Situation
- Method to assess strength of attachment.
- Conducted in a novel environment.
- Involves 8 episodes.
- Infant's behaviour observed as mother leaves and returns, and when a stranger is present.
- Measures attachment in terms of stranger anxiety and separation anxiety.

Stranger anxiety
- Distress shown by an infant when approached by an unfamiliar person.

Secure and insecure attachment

keySTUDY Ainsworth et al. (1978)

How? The **Strange Situation** (a **controlled observation**). Infant and parent placed in a novel ('strange') environment, with a stranger. Their interactions in 8 episodes were observed, for example parent leaves child, child on own with a stranger, parent returns. The study involved 106 middle-class US infants. A team of observers recorded infant's responses to each episode.

Showed? Distinct behaviour patterns identified:
- 66% of infants displayed **secure attachment** (willing to explore, high stranger anxiety, easy to soothe, enthusiastic reunion).
- 22% were **insecure-avoidant** (willing to explore, low stranger anxiety, indifferent to parent's departure, avoid contact on reunion).
- 12% were **insecure-resistant** (not willing to explore, high stranger anxiety, distressed by parent's departure, seek/reject contact on reunion).

Research evidence

Caregiver sensitivity – **Naturalistic observation** of 26 infants in Uganda by **Ainsworth** (1967). The mothers who were more sensitive to their infants' needs had more securely attached infants (infants cried less and explored more). These results can't be explained by **learning theory** but could be explained within Bowlby's theory.

Disorganised attachment – **Main and Solomon** analysed videotapes of children in the Strange Situation and identified this fourth attachment type: infants would show very strong attachment behaviour one minute, followed by avoidance or looking fearful towards their caregiver.

Disinhibited attachment results from **privation**. Infants try to form attachments with anyone they meet, but such attachments are superficial.

Evaluation

Validity – what is being measured? The Strange Situation does not actually measure a personality quality in an individual – it measures the way two people (an adult and an infant) interact, i.e. one attachment relationship. Attachment type may be a sum of many different attachment relationships. However, **Main and Weston** found that attachment type is mainly influenced by the mother, i.e. that one relationship determines overall attachment type.

Effects of attachment type (predictive validity) – We would expect securely attached infants to have better emotional and social development (**continuity hypothesis**). **Hazan and Shaver** supported this, finding that people classified as securely attached in early life, later were more trusting and more likely to form lasting relationships.

Sensitivity – Ainsworth found, as she had predicted, that mothers of securely attached infants were more sensitive, accepting, cooperative and accessible. This suggests that sensitivity leads to secure attachment. However **maternal reflexive thinking** has been found to be more important than sensitivity in establishing secure attachment (**Slade et al.**).

PUTTING IT ALL TOGETHER

The concepts of secure and insecure attachment have led to useful insights into infant and adult behaviour, and provide an understanding of how parenting practices can be improved.

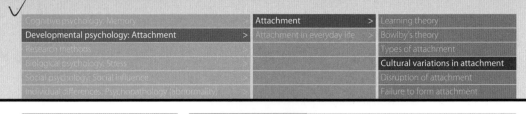

		Attachment	>	Learning theory
Cognitive psychology: Memory		Attachment in everyday life	>	Bowlby's theory
Developmental psychology: Attachment	>			Types of attachment
Research methods				**Cultural variations in attachment**
Biological psychology: Stress				Disruption of attachment
Social psychology: Social influence	>			Failure to form attachment
Individual differences: Psychopathology (abnormality)	>			

KEY TERMS

Culture
- The rules, customs, morals and ways of interacting that bind together members of a society or collection of people.

Collectivist culture
- Any culture that places more value on the 'collective' rather than the individual.
- And on interdependence rather than independence.
- The opposite is true of **individualist culture**.

Imposed etic
- A technique or theory that is developed in one culture and then used to study the behaviour of people in a different culture.
- Such a technique or theory may be meaningless when used with people who have had different experiences or have different values.

⟳ PUTTING IT ALL TOGETHER

Prior and Glaser conclude that expressions of maternal sensitivity and manifestations of secure-base behaviour may vary across cultures, but the core concepts are universal.

Cultural variations

⬡ Cultural similarities

If **attachment** processes are innate (as Bowlby suggested), we would expect to find similarities (called 'universals') across cultures.

Ainsworth's Ugandan study (see page 25) found various universals in attachment behaviour, e.g. mothers of infants with **secure attachment** showed greater sensitivity towards their infants than mothers of infants with **insecure attachment**.

Tronick et al. observed members of the Efe, from Zaire (see page 24). Despite using childrearing practices that are quite different from those in Western **individualist cultures**, at 6 months the infants still showed one primary attachment.

Fox observed infants raised on Israeli kibbutzim in communal children's homes. Infants showed greater attachment to their mothers despite spending more time with the *metapelets* (community nurses), presumably because their mothers showed greater sensitivity.

Van IJzendoorn and Kroonenberg conducted a **meta-analysis** of 32 studies. Variations within cultures were 1.5 times greater than between cultures, suggesting that cultural practices have little influence on attachment behaviour.

⬡ Cultural differences

If cultural differences in attachment are observed, this suggests that culturally-determined childrearing practices (rather than inherited processes) affect attachment.

Grossmann and Grossmann found that a larger proportion of German infants tended to be classified as insecurely, rather than securely, attached than found in the US samples.

Takahashi found that Japanese infants showed much higher rates of **insecure-resistant attachment** (32%) than in most other cultures, and no evidence of **insecure-avoidant attachment**.

⬡ Evaluation

Culture bias – Rothbaum et al. argued that attachment theory has a strong Western bias, reflecting **individualist** ideas of the importance of autonomy. In **collectivist** societies, such as Japan, carers' sensitivity leads to dependence, inhibition of emotional expression and less desire to explore.

Indigenous theories – Rothbaum et al. argue that attachment theories should be rooted in indigenous cultures, but **Posada and Jacobs** believe that there is good evidence to support universality of core concepts.

Nation versus culture – Within any country there are many cultures, yet most research refers to countries such as Japan or America. Such research may lack validity because many different cultural groups, each with different childrearing methods, have been lumped together. Therefore it is does not make sense to claim an association between a country and the attachment types within that country because each country uses many different childrearing methods.

Cross-cultural similarities may be explained by universally shared mass media (e.g. TV and books) rather than by innate processes.

Cross-cultural research involves the use of **imposed etics** making the findings meaningless. For example, Japanese infants are rarely separated from their mothers so their apparent distress on separation during the Strange Situation is not because of insecure attachment, but because they are never separated.

- Germans like enter personal space

Cognitive psychology: Memory	**Attachment** >	Learning theory
Developmental psychology: Attachment >	Attachment in everyday life >	Bowlby's theory
Research methods		Types of attachment
Biological psychology: Stress		Cultural variations in attachment
Social psychology: Social influence		**Disruption of attachment**
Individual differences: Psychopathology (abnormality)		Failure to form attachment

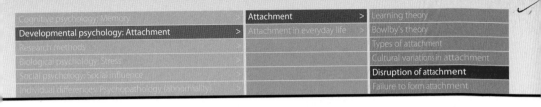

KEY TERM

Disruption of attachment

- Occurs when a child is separated from their primary attachment figure.
- Physical separation may not necessarily result in disruption of attachment if emotional support is maintained.

⏱ PUTTING IT ALL TOGETHER

The research shows a clear difference between physical and emotional disruption. When children experience physical separation from their primary attachment figure, the resulting disruption of attachment does not have negative effects *as long as* alternative emotional care is provided.

However, such children may be more vulnerable in later life when having to cope with stressful situations.

Disruption of attachment

Bowlby's theory predicted that disruption of **attachment** in early life is likely to have a negative effect on social and emotional development.

Spitz and Wolf observed that 100 'normal' children who were placed in an institution became severely depressed within a few months of being placed there.

💡 keySTUDY Robertson and Robertson (1963–1973)

How? Naturalistic observations recorded in films. Six children (aged less than 3) were studied during periods of brief separation from their **primary attachment figure**: Laura was in hospital; John was in a residential nursery; and Jane, Lucy, Thomas and Kate were looked after by the Robinsons in their home where they received a high level of substitute emotional care.

Showed? Laura and John became depressed and withdrawn. The other children coped well and returned to their families happily. *Physical* separation, as in the cases of Jane, Lucy, Thomas and Kate, did not have a negative outcome because substitute emotional care was offered. In contrast, the *emotional* disruption experienced by Laura and John did appear to have negative consequences.

Validity? These were **case studies** of unique individuals and situations, which means they may lack generalisability. However, the data collected was rich in detail.

⬡ Evaluation

Emotional versus physical disruption shown in Robertson's research, and supported **Skeels and Dye**, who found that a group of institutionalised children with low IQs later improved after they were transferred to a home for mentally retarded adults (substitute emotional care). This was then tested by **Skodak and Skeels**. One group of infants in institutional care was transferred to a home for mentally retarded adults, while a control group remained in the orphanage. After 1.5 years the IQs of the control group had fallen whereas the transferred group's IQs had risen from 64 to 92 points.

Reversing emotional disruption – Bohman and Sigvardsson studied over 600 adopted children in Sweden. At the age of 11, 26% of them were classified as 'problem children'. Ten years later, after successful adoptions, they were the same as 'normal' children in terms of social and emotional development.

Role of triggers – Bifulco et al. studied 249 women who had lost mothers through separation or death before they were 17. This group was twice as likely to suffer from **depression** or **anxiety** disorders when they became adults. This suggests that early disruptions in attachment may make an individual psychologically more vulnerable and, if triggered by stressful events later in life, mental disorders may develop.

Individual differences – There is an interaction between security of attachment and the effects of attachment disruption – children who are **securely attached** appear to cope better with disruption. **Bowlby et al.** studied children who were in institutional care (a TB sanatorium) when young. Some of the children were later quite well adjusted, whereas others were maladjusted – Bowlby et al. suggested that those who coped better may have been securely attached.

Deprivation
Privation
Institutionalisation

Cognitive psychology: Memory		Attachment	>	Learning theory
Developmental psychology: Attachment	>	Attachment in everyday life	>	Bowlby's theory
Research methods				Types of attachment
Biological psychology: Stress				Cultural variations in attachment
Social psychology: Social influence				Disruption of attachment
Individual differences: Psychopathology (abnormality)				**Failure to form attachment**

KEY TERMS

Attachment disorder

- A psychiatric disorder characterised by an individual's inability to identify a preferred **attachment** figure.
- Individuals typically show an inability to interact and relate to others, evident before the age of 5.
- Individuals may lack a conscience and be unable to trust others or form lasting relationships.

Deprivation dwarfism

- Children who experience emotional deprivation are often physically smaller.
- Emotional disturbance (stress) may affect the production of **hormones**, such as growth hormones, and lead to a kind of 'dwarfism'.

Institutional care

- An institution is a place dedicated to a particular task.
- Children live there for a period of time.
- Many institutions are unable to offer emotional care.

Privation

- The failure to develop any attachments during early life.
- This is contrasted with 'deprivation' or 'disruption' where attachment bonds have formed, but may be disrupted. Such disruption may last for weeks or a lifetime (in the case of parental death).

Failure to form attachment (privation)

keySTUDY Hodges and Tizard (1989)

How? Longitudinal **natural experiment**. They followed a group of 65 children placed in **institutional care** when less than 4 months old. Caregivers in the home were told not to form attachments with the children.

Showed? At age 16 those children who had been adopted were closely attached to their families, which was not true of the children who had returned to their natural families. However both groups of ex-institutional children had problems with peers (e.g. were less likely to have a best friend) and sought more attention from adults (a sign of **disinhibited attachment**).

Other research evidence

Romanian orphans (institutional care) – **Rutter et al.** conducted a **longitudinal study** of a group of about 100 Romanian orphans adopted by UK families. The children who were adopted by British families before the age of 6 months showed 'normal' emotional development. However, many of the Romanian orphans adopted after 6 months showed disinhibited attachments and had problems with peers.

Attachment disorder is likely to be caused by the experience of severe neglect or frequent change of caregivers in early life. Individuals with attachment disorder may be *reactive/inhibited* (withdrawn, unable to cope with most social situations) or *disinhibited* (overfriendly and attention-seeking).

Case studies of isolated children (privation but not institutional care)

1 **Genie** was locked in a room by her father until she was 13½). She never fully recovered socially and lacked social responsiveness. Her lack of recovery may be due to privation or may be due to being retarded, or because of the physical deprivation she experienced (**Rymer**).

2 The **Czech twins** spent the first 7 years of their lives locked up by a stepmother and were unable to talk when found. They were then well cared for by two loving sisters and, by age 14, had near-normal intellectual and social functioning. By the age of 20, they were of above average intelligence and had excellent relationships with members of their foster family (**Koluchová**).

Evaluation

Poor parenting – **Quinton et al.** found that ex-institutional women often had difficulties as parents, creating a cycle of **privation**. More of the ex-institutional women were rated as lacking in warmth when interacting with their children and had children who have spent time in care.

Deprivation dwarfism – **Gardner** recorded case studies, such as one girl who, from birth, had to be fed through a tube. Her mother never cuddled the girl, in fear of dislodging the tube. By 8 months old, the child was severely withdrawn and physically stunted. When admitted to hospital, she was given lots of attention and soon returned to normal, despite no change in her diet.

Privation is only one factor – Some of the Romanian orphans did recover. In those who didn't recover the damage was probably due to multiple risk factors such as late adoption, particular hardship in the institutions and lower personal resilience.

Privation or rejection? In Hodges and Tizard's study the effects might be due to rejection and we also don't know whether, in the long term, they might have recovered as long-term follow-ups were not possible.

PUTTING IT ALL TOGETHER

This research suggests that children who *lack* early attachments are likely to experience permanent emotional and social difficulties later in life, though these effects may be less severe if subsequent emotional care is given.

Cognitive psychology: Memory	>	Attachment	>	The impact of day care
Developmental psychology: Attachment	>	Attachment in everyday life	>	Implications for child care practices
Research methods				
Biological psychology: Stress				
Social psychology: Social influence				
Individual differences: Psychopathology (abnormality)				

Impact of day care on aggressiveness

⬡ Negative effects

The **NICHD** study is a **longitudinal study** conducted in the US since 1991, involving over 1000 children from diverse families and locations. At age 5, children who had been in day care of any kind were rated as more assertive, disobedient and aggressive. Children in full-time day care (more than 30 hours) were about three times more likely to show behaviour problems (e.g. arguing, temper tantrums, lying and hitting) compared with those cared for by their mothers at home.

The EPPE study in the UK has found similar results to NICHD. Involves 3000 children aged 3–7 years in a variety of day care settings. Children who spent longer in day care were rated by teachers as more aggressive and disobedient. This was particularly true of children in day care centres where many start before the age of 2. High quality day care associated with less impact (**Sylva et al.**).

⬡ Evaluation

Reinterpreting the NICHD results – These can also be used to show that day care is *not* necessarily associated with aggressiveness; 83% of children attending **day care** for less than 30 hours per week did *not* show higher levels of aggression (**Friedman**). This underlies the importance of looking carefully at the findings.

Other factors affect aggression – NICHD data also showed that a mother's sensitivity to her child was a better indicator of reported problem behaviours than was time in child care (less sensitivity = more problem behaviours).

Lack of causal relationship – Research does not demonstrate that day care has *caused* any later behaviours – only **correlations** have been demonstrated. **Dingfelder** suggests that we need to better understand the processes, e.g. what particular elements of day care may lead to negative outcomes?

⬡ Mediating factors

- **Quality of care** – low quality care associated with poor social development (**NICHD**).
- **Lack of commitment** – Parents have greater interest in their child and thus inevitably show greater involvement. **Bryant et al.** found fewer secure attachment links with day care staff than with parents.
- **Individual differences** – shy children may find day care more difficult (**Pennebaker et al.**).
- **Child's age** – Children who start day care before 18 months are more likely to show negative effects (**Gregg et al.**).
- **Number of hours** – Children who attend day care full-time may show more negative effects, although **Clarke-Stewart et al.** found no difference related to the number of hours spent in day care.

KEY TERMS

Day care
- A form of temporary care (i.e. not all day and night).
- Not provided by parents.
- Usually takes place outside the home.

Impact of day care on peer relations

⬡ Negative effects

Attachment – Secure attachment is better for peer relations. **Sroufe et al.** linked insecure attachment to greater difficulty with peer relations. **Belsky and Rovine** found that children who had received 20 hours or more of day care per week before they were 1 year old were more likely to be **insecurely attached** compared with children at home.

Social development – Clarke-Stewart et al. studied 150 children and found that those who were in day care were consistently more advanced in their social development than children who stayed home with mothers. These advances were in social development, independence, dinnertime obedience, compliance requests and social interaction with peers.

Social strategies – Field conducted a correlational study and found a **positive correlation** between the amount of time spent in full-time day care and the number of friends a child had once they went to school.

⬡ Evaluation

Lack of causal relationship – Other factors may explain the link between day care and increased sociability. For example, mothers who are shy by nature may prefer to stay at home and look after their children. Their children may have inherited a similar temperament, therefore it is mainly socially outgoing children who go to day care.

⬡ Day care has no effects

Day care is not the only influence on a child's development. It is difficult to disentangle the direct effects of day care from other factors, e.g. the type of attachment between mother and child. **Clarke-Stewart** concluded that, while day care programmes may have some direct effects on development, they clearly were not operating alone.

↻ PUTTING IT ALL TOGETHER

There is evidence for both positive and negative effects of day care, or no effects at all. A child's development is influenced by an array of different factors, only one of which is day care.

Cognitive psychology: Memory	>	Attachment	>	The impact of day care	
Developmental psychology: Early social development	>	Attachment in everyday life	>	Implications for child care practices	
Research methods	>				
Biological psychology: Stress	>				
Social psychology: Social influence	>				
Individual differences: Psychotherapy (abnormality)	>				

Influence of attachment research

Improving quality of day care – The potential negative effects may be countered by recognising the role of day care workers as attachment figures. The Soho Family Centre in London bases its day care programme on attachment theory. Each carer is assigned a maximum of three children and is paired with another carer who can step in if need be, thus ensuring close and consistent emotional relationships.

Institutional care (such as hospitals and adoption centres) – Attachment research recommends the provision of substitute emotional care to counter the effects of physical separation.

Adoption – Late adoptions used to be encouraged so the infant's biological mother had time to nurse the baby, but then the sensitive period for attachment had passed by the time an adoption was made. Today, most babies are adopted within the first week of birth and research shows that adoptive mothers and children are just as securely attached as non-adoptive families (**Singer et al.**).

Improving the quality of parenting – Parents who had poor attachment experiences themselves may need assistance to learn parenting skills. The 'Circle of Security' programme (**Cooper et al.**) teaches caregivers to respond more sensitively.

Evaluation

Improving the quality of day care – Supported by **Bowlby**'s theory and the importance of secondary attachment figures.

Institutional care – Supported by **Robertson and Robertson** (see page 27) who showed that negative effects of disruption could be avoided with substitute emotional care.

Adoption – Supported by **Hodges and Tizard** (see page 28) who showed that failure to form attachment can have long-term consequences.

Improving the quality of parenting – Research by **Quinton et al.** (see page 28) showed that poor parenting may be related to parents' own childhood experiences.

Influence of day care research

Importance of high-quality day care – Low-quality care is associated with negative effects (e.g. increased aggression). High-quality care is associated with benefits from day care (e.g. increased sociability). Sensitive care is an important ingredient.

Good staff-to-child ratios – The **NICHD** study found that its day care staff could only provide sensitive care if the ratios were as low as 1:3.

Minimal staff turnover – When staff come and go, children may either fail to form attachments to them or, if they have formed an attachment, they suffer the anxiety associated with disruption of attachment when the staff leave (**Schaffer**).

Qualified and experienced staff – **Sylva et al.** found that quality was associated with the qualification levels of the day care staff.

Evaluation

Importance of high-quality day care – Supported by both **Bowlby** and **Ainsworth** who suggested that sensitivity of care was important for healthy, secure attachments. The factors listed above have all been shown to produce high-quality sensitive care.

Problems associated with day care may be due to low-quality care. The **NICHD** study found that about 23% of infant day care providers gave 'highly' sensitive infant care whereas 20% were 'emotionally detached' from the infants under their care.

PUTTING IT ALL TOGETHER

It is clear that psychological research into attachment and day care has had, and continues to have, an important effect on the way we look after children both in their own homes and when they need to be cared for outside the home.

SCHWADRon

"IT WAS A GREAT IDEA to OPEN A DAY CARE CENTER FOR KIDS WHOSE PARENTS ARE HUNTING AND GATHERING."

Chapter 3

Research methods

Column 1: tick when you have produced brief notes.

Column 2: tick when you have a good grasp of this topic.

Column 3: tick during the final revision when you feel you have complete mastery of the topic.

Key terms/concepts • What, how and why (advantages and limitations)	1	2	3
Experimental method • Laboratory, field, natural • Experimental design (independent groups, repeated measures, and matched pairs) • Advantages and limitations			
Studies using a correlational analysis • Analysis and interpretation of correlational data • Positive and negative correlations • Interpretation of correlation coefficients • Advantages and limitations			
Observational techniques • Design of naturalistic observations • Development and use of behavioural categories • Advantages and limitations			
Self-report techniques • Design of questionnaires and interviews • Advantages and limitations			
Case studies • Advantages and limitations			
Validity • Control of extraneous variables • Demand characteristics and investigator effects • How to deal with low validity			
Reliability • How to deal with low reliability			
Ethical issues • Ways in which psychologists deal with them • Awareness of the BPS Code of Ethics			
Selection of participants • Sampling techniques including random, opportunity and volunteer sampling			
Aims and hypotheses • Including directional and non-directional			
Operationalisation of variables • Including independent and dependent variables			
Pilot studies			
Quantitative data, presentation and interpretation • Graphs, scattergrams and tables • Measures of central tendency including median, mean, mode • Measures of dispersion including ranges and standard deviation			
Qualitative data, analysis and presentation • Processes involved in content analysis			

Cognitive psychology: Memory		Methods and techniques	>	Advantages and limitations
Developmental psychology: Attachment	>	Investigation design	>	
Research methods	>	Data analysis		
Biological psychology: Stress		and presentation	>	
Social psychology: Social influence	>			
Individual differences: Psychopathology (abnormality)	>			

Method/technique		Nature and use	Advantages and limitations
Experiments	**Lab experiment**	**IV** manipulated to observe effect on **DV**, highly controlled.	+ Can draw causal **conclusion**. + **Extraneous variables** minimised. + Can be easily replicated. − Contrived, tends to lack **mundane realism**. − **Investigator** and **participant effects**.
	Field experiment	More natural (or ordinary) surroundings, IV directly manipulated by experimenter to observe effect on DV, some control.	+ Can draw causal conclusion. + Usually higher **ecological validity**. + Avoids some **participant effects**. − Less control. − May have **demand characteristics**.
	Natural experiment	IV not directly manipulated, it is one that would vary anyway. Participants not randomly allocated.	+ Allows research where the IV can't be manipulated for ethical/ practical reasons. + Enables psychologists to study 'real' problems. − Cannot demonstrate causal relationships. − Inevitably many **extraneous variables**. − **Investigator** and **participant effects**.
Studies using a correlational analysis		**Co-variables** examined for positive, negative or zero association.	+ Can be used when not possible to manipulate variables. + Can rule out a causal relationship. − People often misinterpret correlations. − There may be other, unknown variables.
Observational techniques	**Naturalistic observation**	Everything left as normal, all variables free to vary.	+ Study behaviour where can't manipulate variables. + High **ecological validity**. − Poor control of **extraneous variables**. − **Observer bias** − Low **inter-observer reliability** can be a problem.
	Controlled observation	Some variables controlled by researcher, e.g. the environment.	+ Can manipulate variables to observe effects. − Less natural, reduced **ecological validity** can be a problem. − **Investigator** and **participant effects**. − **Observer bias** − Low **inter-observer reliability** can be a problem.
	Content analysis	Indirect observation of behaviour based on written or verbal material such as interviews or TV.	+ High **ecological validity** because based on what people do. + Can be replicated easily because sources are publicly available. − **Observer bias**. − Low **inter-observer reliability** can be a problem.
Self-report techniques	**Questionnaires**	Set of written questions.	+ Can be easily repeated, so lots of people can be questioned. + Respondents may be more willing to reveal personal information. + Does not require specialist administrators. − **Leading questions, social desirability bias**. −· Biased samples.
	Interviews	**Unstructured interviews** where the interviewer develops questions in response to respondent's answers, conducted in real time.	+ More detailed information collected through in-depth questioning. + Can access unexpected information. − **Social desirability bias, interviewer bias, inter-interviewer reliability, leading questions**. − Requires well-trained personnel.
Case studies		Detailed study of a single individual, institution or event. Involves many different techniques, e.g. interviews, psychological tests.	+ Rich, in-depth data collected. + Used to investigate unusual instances of behaviour. + Complex interactions studied. − Lacks generalisability. − May involve unreliable, retrospective recall. − Researcher may lack objectivity.

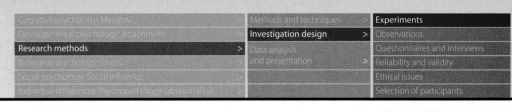

Cognitive psychology: Memory	>	Methods and techniques	>	Experiments
Developmental psychology: Attachment		Investigation design	>	Observations
Research methods	>	Data analysis		Questionnaires and interviews
Biological psychology: Stress	>	and presentation	>	Reliability and validity
Social psychology: Social influence	>			Ethical issues
Individual differences: Psychopathology (abnormality)	>			Selection of participants

Designing experiments

⬡ Independent and dependent variables

Independent variable (IV) is an event that is directly manipulated by the experimenter in order to observe its effects on the DV.

Dependent variable (DV) depends in some way on the IV.

Variables must be **operationalised**, i.e. defined in a way that they can be tested. For example, instead of a DV 'educational attainment', an experimenter must specify a way to measure this, such as GCSE grades.

⬡ Aims and hypotheses

The **aim** of any study is a statement of what the researcher intends to investigate. A **hypothesis** is a precise and testable (operationalised) statement about the expected relationship between variables.

A hypothesis may be **directional** where it states the direction of the predicted difference or relationship between two conditions or two groups of participants. Or it may be **non-directional**, simply predicting that there will be a difference or relationship between two conditions or two groups of participants, without stating the direction.

⬡ Experimental design

A set of procedures used to control the influence of factors such as **participant variables** in an experiment.

Repeated measures	
Same participants in every condition being tested.	+ Good control for participant variables. + Fewer participants needed. – **Order effects** (e.g. boredom, practice). – Participants may guess the purpose of the experiment.

Independent groups	
Participants are allocated to two (or more) groups representing different experimental conditions.	+ Avoids order effects and participants guessing the purpose of the experiment. – Needs more participants. – No control of participant variables (can use **random allocation**).

Matched pairs	
Pairs of participants matched on key participant variables. One member of each pair is placed in the experimental group and the other member in the control group.	+ Avoids order effects. + Participant variables partly controlled. – Matching is difficult and never totally successful.

Counterbalancing can be used to deal with order effects by ensuring that each condition is tested first or second in equal amounts.
- Some participants receive condition A then B, others receive B then A.
- Or ABBA – all participants receive A B then B A.

Groups and conditions

In an experiment using a **repeated measures** or **matched pairs design** each participant takes part in two or more conditions. The **experimental condition** (or conditions) contains the independent variable. The **control condition** provides a baseline measure of behaviour without the experimental treatment (IV), so that the effect of the experimental treatment may be assessed.

In an experiment using an **independent groups design**, there is an **experimental group** and a **control group.**

Demand characteristics
- A cue that makes participants aware of what the researcher expects to find or how participants are expected to behave.

Extraneous variable (EV)
- Any variable, other than the IV, which may potentially affect the DV and thereby confound the findings.
- Order effects, participant variables and situational variables may act as EVs.

Order effects
- In a repeated measures design, an extraneous variable arising from the order in which conditions are presented.
- For example, a **practice effect**.

Random allocation
- Allocating participants to experimental groups using random techniques.

⬡ Control of variables

'Control' refers to the extent to which any variable is held constant or regulated by a researcher. The IV is controlled to observe its effect. EVs are controlled so any effect can be attributed to the IV, for example:

- **Participant variables** such as age, intelligence, motivation, etc. may explain why participants in one group do better.
- **Situational variables** such as time of day, temperature, noise, etc. may also explain group differences.
- **Investigator effects**, where the investigator directly or indirectly has an effect on a participant's performance, other than what was intended.
- **Demand characteristics** trigger a predictable response.

Methods of control include:

- **Single blind technique** – Participants don't know the true aims of a study.
- **Double blind technique** – Investigators and participants don't know the true aims of a study.

Cognitive psychology: Memory		Methods and techniques	>	Experiments
Developmental psychology: Attachment		Investigation design	>	Observations
Research methods	>	Data analysis		Questionnaires and interviews
Biological psychology: Stress	>	and presentation	>	Reliability and validity
Social psychology: Social Influence				Ethical issues
Individual differences: Psychopathology (abnormality)	>			Selection of participants

Observational design

Behavioural categories

It is necessary to devise objective methods to separate the continuous stream of action into separate **behavioural categories**, i.e. **operationalise** the target behaviour(s). This can be done using:

- **Behaviour checklist** – A list of component behaviours.
- **Coding system** – Individual behaviours are given a code for ease of recording.

The behavioural categories should:

- Be *objective* – The observer should not have to make inferences about the behaviour.
- Cover *all possible component behaviours* and avoid a 'waste basket' category.
- Be *mutually exclusive*, meaning that you should not have to mark two categories at one time.

Sampling procedures

In many situations, continuous observation is not possible because there would be too much data to record, therefore there must be a systematic method of **sampling** observations:

- **Event sampling** – Counting the number of times a certain behaviour (event) occurs in a target individual.
- **Time sampling** – Recording behaviours at regular intervals, e.g. every 30 seconds or some other time interval.

Participant and non-participant

In some observations, the observer is also a participant in the behaviour being observed (**participant observation**) which is likely to affect objectivity. More often, the observer is not a participant (**non-participant observation**).

Overt and covert

Participants who are aware of being observed (**overt observation**) may alter their behaviour, so **validity** is reduced. Making observations without a participant's knowledge (**covert observations**), such as using one-way mirrors, may raise **ethical issues**.

Structured and unstructured

In a **structured observation** the observer uses behavioural categories and sampling procedures to structure the observations. In a **controlled observation** both the observations and the environment are controlled (structured); in a **naturalistic observation** only the observations are structured.

In an **unstructured observation** the observer records all relevant behaviour but has no system.

KEY TERMS
Pilot study

- A small-scale trial of a study.
- Small group of participants run through the procedures.
- Aims to test any aspects of the design, with a view to making improvements.

Questionnaires and interviews

Good questions

A 'good question' should be clear and unambiguous. It should not be biased in a way that might suggest particular answers to the respondent (i.e. a **leading question**).

Closed questions have a range of answers from which respondents select one.

+ They produce **quantitative data** which is easier to analyse.

– Respondents may be forced to select answers that don't represent their real thoughts or behaviour.

Open questions invite respondents to provide their own answers rather than select one of those provided. They tend to produce **qualitative data**.

+ Can provide unexpected answers and rich detail, allowing researchers to gain new insights.

– More difficult to summarise answers because there may be such a wide variety of responses. This then makes it difficult to draw **conclusions**.

Good questionnaires/interviews

Questions should be unthreatening and easy to answer. More challenging questions will be answered more truthfully once trust is established.

Filler questions may be used that disguise the true aims of the **questionnaire/interview** so that respondents are more honest.

Sampling techniques are important in obtaining a representative sample.

A **pilot study** enables questions to be tested on a small group of people. This means you can refine the questions in response to any difficulties encountered.

Structured and unstructured

In a **structured interview** the questions are decided in advance and are the same for all participants.

In an **unstructured interview** the questions are unplanned and usually guided by the respondents' answers.

In a **clinical interview** (semi-structured) the interviewer starts with a few standard questions but further questions develop in response to the answers given.

Cognitive psychology: Memory	>	Methods and techniques	>	Experiments
Developmental psychology: Attachment		Investigation design	>	Observations
Research methods	>	Data analysis		Questionnaires and interviews
Biological psychology: Stress		and presentation	>	**Reliability and validity**
Social psychology: Social influence	>			Ethical issues
Individual differences: Psychopathology (abnormality)	>			Selection of participants

 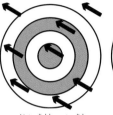 

Reliable, but not valid	Not reliable, not valid	Reliable and valid

Reliability

Experimental studies – The reliability of an experiment can be determined through replication.

- *To improve reliability* **extraneous variables** should be controlled.

Observational studies – **Inter-observer reliability** is the extent to which there is agreement between two or more observers.

- *To assess internal reliability* – Correlate the observations of two or more observers. If (total number of agreements) / (total number of observations) > .80, the data has high inter-observer reliability.
- *To improve reliability* observers trained to use **behavioural categories**.

Self-report techniques – **Inter-interviewer reliability** is the extent to which two interviewers produce the same outcome from an interview.

- *To assess internal reliability* the **split-half method** can be used. Scores/responses on both halves of a test should be the same/consistent.
- *To assess external reliability* the **test-retest method** can be used when the same questionnaire/interview is repeated with the same respondent a few weeks apart.
- *To improve reliability* – remove questions which create inconsistency.

KEY TERMS

Reliability
- A measure of consistency.
- **Internal reliability** concerns consistency *within* a set of scores or items.
- **External reliability** concerns consistency *over time* such that it is possible to obtain the same results on subsequent occasions when the measure is used with the same thing.

Validity
- The extent to which a study and its findings are legitimate or true.
- **Internal validity** concerns whether a study has tested what it set out to test.
- **External validity** concerns the degree to which a research finding can be generalised to, for example, other settings (**ecological validity**), or other groups of people (**population validity**) and over time (**historical validity**).
- Any study that has low internal validity must lack generalisability and therefore also has low external validity.

Validity

Experimental studies

- *Internal validity* – The degree to which the observed effect was due to experimental manipulation rather than factors such as extraneous variables. It is also affected by **mundane realism** and **experimental realism**.
- *External validity* – The representativeness of the sample affects the ability to generalise the findings to other people and situations (i.e. **population validity** and **ecological validity**).

Observational studies

- *Internal validity* may be affected by an inadequate system of behavioural categories (e.g. not enough categories) and by **observer bias** (observers' expectations affect their objectivity).
- *Improving internal validity* – Use more than one observer in more than one setting.
- *External validity* – **Naturalistic observations** are likely to have high ecological validity but would have low population validity if the sample is limited.

Self-report techniques

- *Internal validity* may be affected by **interviewer bias** and **social desirability bias**.
- *Improving validity* – Use a more representative **sampling** method and better designed questions.
- *Assessing validity* – Compare the results with an established measure of the same thing (called **concurrent validity**).
- *External validity* – The representativeness of the sample affects the ability to generalise the findings to other people and situations (population validity and ecological validity).

Cognitive psychology: Memory	>	Methods and techniques	>	Experiments
Developmental psychology: Attachment		Investigation design	>	Observations
Research methods	>	Data analysis		Questionnaires and interviews
Biological psychology: Stress		and presentation	>	Reliability and validity
Social psychology: Social influence	>			Ethical issues
Individual differences: Psychopathology (abnormality)	>			Selection of participants

Ethical issues

Informed consent

- Participants must be given comprehensive information concerning the nature and purpose of a study and their role in it.
- Using this information, participants can make an informed decision about whether to participate.
- From the researcher's point of view this may reduce the meaningfulness of the research because such information will reveal the study's aims and affect participants' behaviour.

Deception

- This occurs when a participant is not told the true aims of a study and what participation will involve.
- Thus the participants cannot give informed consent.
- From the researcher's point of view it might be argued that some deception is relatively harmless and/or can be compensated for by **debriefing**.

Right to withdraw

- Participants should have the right to withdraw from a study if they feel uncomfortable in any way.
- They should also have the right to refuse the researcher permission to use any data they produce.
- From the researcher's point of view the loss of participants may bias the study's findings.

Protection from harm

- During a research study, participants should not experience negative physical effects, such as physical injury, or psychological effects, such as lowered self-esteem or embarrassment.
- From the researcher's point of view it may not be possible to estimate harm before conducting a study – however any study should be stopped as soon as harm is apparent.

Confidentiality (and anonymity)

- A participant's right to have personal information protected.
- The Data Protection Act makes confidentiality a legal right.
- From the researcher's point of view it may not be possible to keep information confidential because details of the study lead to individual's identification.

Privacy

- A person's right to control the flow of information about themselves.
- From the researcher's point of view this may be difficult, for example in a **covert observation**.
- If privacy is invaded, confidentiality should be protected.

Dealing with ethical issues

Debriefing

- A post-research interview designed to inform participants about the true nature of a study.
- This aims to restore participants to the state they were in at the start of the study.
- It may also be used to gain feedback about the procedures used in the study.

Ethical guidelines

- Concrete, quasi-legal documents that help to conduct within psychology.
- Establish principles for standard practice and competence.
- Published by professional organisations such as the *Code of Conduct* produced by the BPS (British Psychological Society).

Ethical committee (also called institutional review board, IRB)

- A group of people within a research institution that must approve a study before it begins.
- May consist of professionals and lay people.
- Considers how the researcher proposes to deal with any ethical issues that arise.
- Weighs up cost-benefit issues.

Presumptive consent

- A method of dealing with lack of informed consent or deception.
- Asking a group of people who are similar to the participants whether they would agree to take part in a study.
- If this group of people agree to the procedures in the proposed study, it is presumed that the real participants would agree as well.

Cognitive psychology: Memory		Methods and techniques	>	Experiments
Developmental psychology: Attachment		**Investigation design**	>	Observations
Research methods	>	Data analysis		Questionnaires and interviews
Biological psychology: Stress	>	and presentation	>	Reliability and validity
Social psychology: Social influence	>			Ethical issues
Individual differences: Psychopathology (abnormality)	>			Selection of participants

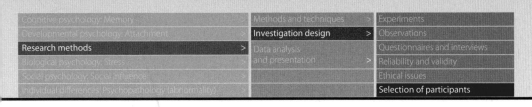

KEY TERMS

Attrition

- The loss of participants from a study over time.
- This is likely to leave a biased sample, or a sample that is too small.

Random technique

- Method of selection that ensures each member of the population has an equal chance of being selected.
- For example, placing all names in a hat and drawing out the required number.
- Or by assigning each person a number and using a random number table.

Sampling

- The process of taking a sample.
- The technique uses aims to produce a representative selection of the target population.

Target population

- The group of people that the researcher is interested in.
- The group of people from whom a sample is drawn.
- The group of people about whom generalisations can be made.

Volunteer bias

- A form of sampling bias.
- Occurs because volunteer participants are usually more highly motivated than randomly selected participants.

Selection of particpants

Opportunity sample A sample of participants produced by selecting people who are most easily available at the time of the study.

How? Ask people in the street, i.e. select those who are available.

+ The easiest method because you just use the first participants you can find, which means it takes less time to locate your sample than if using one of the other techniques.

– Inevitably biased because the sample is drawn from a small part of the **target population**. For example, if you selected your sample from people walking around the centre of a town on a Monday morning, then it would be unlikely to include professional people (because they are at work), or people from rural areas.

Random sample A sample of participants produced using a **random technique** such that every member of the target population has an equal chance of being selected.

How? Using a random technique such as placing all names in a hat and drawing out the required number.

+ Unbiased, all members of the target population have an equal chance of selection.

– The researcher may end up with an unrepresentative and therefore biased sample (e.g. more boys than girls) because not everyone agrees to participate.

Stratified and quota sample Groups of participants are selected according to their frequency in the population.

How? Subgroups (or strata) within a population are identified (e.g. boys and girls, or age groups: 10–12 years, 13–15, etc.). Participants are obtained from each of the strata in proportion to their occurrence in the target population. Selection is done randomly (stratified sample) or by another method such as opportunity sampling (quota sample).

+ More representative than an opportunity sample because there is equal representation of subgroups.

– Although the sample represents subgroups, each quota taken may be biased in other ways, for example, if you use opportunity sampling you only have access to certain sections of the target population.

Systematic sample A method of obtaining a representative sample by selecting every 5th or 10th person.

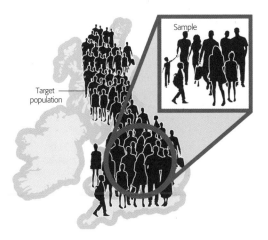

Target population

Sample

How? Use a predetermined system to select participants, such as selecting every 5th, 8th, 10th or whatever person from a phonebook.

+ Unbiased as participants are selected using an objective system.

– Not truly random unless you select a number using a random method and start with this person, and then you select every 5th, 8th, 10th or whatever person.

Volunteer sample A sample of participants produced by asking for volunteers.

How? Advertise in a newspaper or on a noticeboard.

+ Access to a variety of participants (e.g. all the people who read a newspaper) which may make the sample more representative and less biased.

– Sample is biased because participants are likely to be more highly motivated and/or with extra time on their hands (= **volunteer bias**).

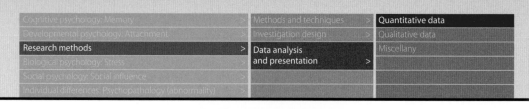

Cognitive psychology: Memory	>	Methods and techniques	>	Quantitative data
Developmental psychology: Attachment	>	Investigation design	>	Qualitative data
Research methods	>	Data analysis and presentation	>	Miscellany
Biological psychology: Stress	>			
Social psychology: Social influence	>			
Individual differences: Psychopathology (abnormality)	>			

KEY TERMS

Quantitative data
- Represent how much, how long, or how many, etc. there are of something.
- Data that are measured in numbers or quantities.

Quantitative data analysis
- Any means of representing trends from numerical data, such as measures of central tendency.

Levels of measurement
- **Nominal** Data is in separate categories, such as grouping people according to their favourite football team.
- **Ordinal** Data is ordered in some way, for example asking people to put a list of football teams in order of liking. The 'difference' between each item is not the same, i.e. the individual may like the first item a lot more than the second, but there might only be a small difference between the items ranked second and third.
- **Interval** Data is measured using units of equal intervals, such as when counting correct answers or using any 'public' unit of measurement.
- **Ratio** There is a true zero point, as in most measures of physical quantities.

Quantitative data analysis

⬡ Measures of central tendency

Measures of central tendency inform us of central (or middle) values for a data set, i.e. the average.

Mean – Calculated by adding up all the numbers and dividing by the number of numbers. It can only be used with **interval** or **ratio** data.

+ Makes use of the values of all the data in the final analysis.

− Can be misrepresentative of the data as a whole if there are extreme values.

Median – The *middle* value in an *ordered* list, suitable for **ordinal** or interval data.

+ Not affected by extreme scores.

− Not always as 'sensitive' as the mean because not all values are reflected (but may sometimes be better if there are extreme scores which unduly affect the mean).

Mode – The value that is *most* common.

+ Useful when the data are in categories, i.e. **nominal** data.

− Not a useful way of describing data when there are several modes (i.e. a multi-modal set of data).

⬡ Measures of dispersion

Measures of dispersion inform us of the spread of the data set.

Range – The difference between the highest and lowest score in a data set.

+ Easy to calculate, provides you with direct information.

− Affected by extreme values, doesn't take into account the number of observations in the data set.

Standard deviation –Shows the amount of variation in a data set and assesses the spread of the data around the mean.

+ More precise measure of dispersion because all the values of the data are taken into account.

− May hide some characteristics of the data, for example extreme values.

⬡ Correlation

A **correlational analysis** determines the extent of a relationship between two co-variables.

Zero correlation – **Co-variables** are not linked at all.

Positive correlation – Co-variables increase together.

Negative correlation – As one co-variable increases, the other decreases.

Usually a linear correlation is predicted, but the relationship can be curvilinear.

Correlation coefficient – A number between −1 and +1 that tells us how closely the co-variables in a correlational analysis are related.

⬡ Visual display

Graphs and tables, such as:

Bar chart – The height of each bar represents the frequency of that item. The categories are placed on the horizontal (*x* axis) and frequency is on the vertical (*y* axis). Bar charts are suitable for words and numbers (nominal or ordinal/interval data).

Scattergram – A graphical representation of the relationship (i.e. the correlation) between two sets of scores.

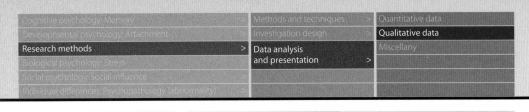

Cognitive psychology: Memory	Methods and techniques	Quantitative data
Developmental psychology: Attachment	Investigation design	**Qualitative data**
Research methods	Data analysis and presentation	Miscellany
Biological psychology: Stress		
Social psychology: Social influence		
Individual differences: Psychopathology (abnormality)		

Qualitative data

- Express the 'quality' of things.
- This includes descriptions, words, meanings, pictures, texts and so on.
- They cannot be counted or quantified but can be turned into **quantitative data** by counting the data in categories.

It is sometimes said that qualitative data concern 'thoughts and feelings' – but you can also have *quantitative* data about thoughts and feelings, for example a researcher could ask participants to rate their feelings about a film on a scale of 1 to 5. The difference between quantitative and qualitative research runs much deeper than 'thoughts and feelings'.

Qualitative data analysis

Qualitative research tends to use smaller *samples* than quantitative research but usually involves the collection of a large amount of data – pages of written material and/or audio/video recordings. Analysis might involve:

1 Categorising the data. These can be:
   - *Pre-existing categories* – The researcher decides on some appropriate categories before beginning the research.
   - *Emergent categories* – The categories or themes emerge when examining the data.

2 Using the categories to summarise the data.
   - The categories or themes may be listed.
   - Examples of behaviour within the category may be represented using quotes from participants or descriptions of typical behaviours in that category.
   - Frequency of occurrences in each category may be counted, thus qualitative data is turned into quantitative data.
   - Finally, a researcher may draw **conclusions**.

Qualitative data versus quantitative data

Strengths	Limitations
Qualitative data	
· Represents the true complexities of human behaviour. · Gains access to thoughts and feelings that may not be assessed using quantitative methods, e.g. **closed questions**. · Provides rich details of how people behave because participants free to express themselves.	· More difficult to detect patterns and draw conclusions because of the large amount of data usually collected. · Subjective analysis can be affected by personal expectations and beliefs – however quantitative methods are also affected by bias; they simply may appear to be objective.
Quantitative data	
· Easier to analyse because the data are given in numbers that can be summarised using measures such as the **mean** and **range**, as well as visually through the use of graphs. · Can produce neat conclusions because numerical data reduces the variety of possibilities.	· Oversimplifies reality and human experience (statistically significant but humanly insignificant).

Processes involved in content analysis

Content analysis is a form of indirect **observation** – indirect because you are not observing people directly but observing them through the artefacts they produce, e.g. videos, books, grafitti, and so on.

The process involved is similar to any observational study, the researcher has to make design decisions about:

1 **Sampling method** – What material to sample and how frequently (e.g. which TV channels to include, how many programmes, what length of time).

2 **Behavioural categories** to be used. These categories can be used in two ways:
   - *Quantitative analysis* – All instances in each category are counted.
   - *Qualitative analysis* – All instances in each category are described rather than counted.

As with observations, if there is a team of researchers it is important to ensure that they are applying criteria in the same way by calculating **inter-observer reliability**.

Cognitive psychology: Memory		Methods and techniques	>	Quantitative data
Developmental psychology: Attachment		Investigation design	>	Qualitative data
Research methods	>	Data analysis and presentation	>	Miscellany
Biological psychology: Stress				
Social psychology: Social influence				
Individual differences: Psychopathology (abnormality)				

Other important research methods topics

Cohort effects One group of participants (cohort) may have unique characteristics because of time-specific experiences during their development, such as being a child during the Second World War. This can affect both **cross-sectional studies** (because one group is not comparable with another) or **longitudinal studies** (because the group studied is not typical).

Conclusions The implications drawn from a study: what the findings tell us about people in general rather than just about the particular participants in a study. Conclusions are used to construct theories.

Confederate An individual in a study who is not a real participant and has been instructed how to behave by the investigator/experimenter. May act as the **independent variable (IV)**.

Cross-cultural study A kind of **natural experiment** in which the IV is different cultural practices and the **DV** is a behaviour, such as attachment. This enables researchers to investigate the effects of culture/socialisation.

Cross-sectional study One group of participants representing one section of society (e.g. young people or working class people) are compared with participants from another group (e.g. old people or middle class people).

Hawthorne effect The tendency for participants to alter their behaviour merely as a result of knowing that they are being observed.

Intervening variable A variable that comes between two other variables that can explain the relationship between those two variables.

Investigator/experimenter bias The effect that an investigator/experimenter's expectations have on the participants and thus on the results of a research study.

Longitudinal study Observation of the same items over a long period of time. Such studies usually aim to compare the same individuals at different ages, in which case the IV is age. A longitudinal study might also observe a school or other institution over a long period of time.

Meta-analysis A researcher looks at the findings from a number of different studies in order to reach a general conclusion about a particular hypothesis.

Quasi-experiments Studies that are 'almost' experiments but lack one or more features of a true experiment, such as full experimenter control over the IV and **random allocation** of participants to conditions. This means that they cannot claim to demonstrate causal relationships.

Role play A **controlled observation** in which participants are asked to imagine how they would behave in certain situations, and then asked to act out the part. This method has the advantage of permitting the study of certain behaviours that might be unethical or difficult to find in the real world.

Standardised procedures A set of procedures that are the same for all participants in order to be able to repeat a study. This includes **standardised instructions** – the instructions given to participants to tell them how to perform a task.

How science works

The **scientific method** is the method used in scientific research where scientists start by observing natural phenomena and then develop explanations and hypotheses which are tested using systematic research methods.

The **experiment** is the ideal scientific method because it lends itself to being objective and highly controlled, but other methods (such as **observations** and **interviews**) can also be objective and controlled.

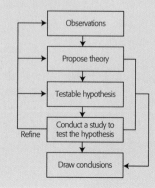

40

Column 1: tick when you have produced brief notes.

Column 2: tick when you have a good grasp of this topic.

Column 3: tick during the final revision when you feel you have complete mastery of the topic.

Key terms • **3 marks' worth of material**	1	2	3
Pituitary-adrenal system			
Sympathomedullary pathway			
Immune system			
Stress-related illness			
Life changes			
Daily hassles			
Workplace stress – workload			
Workplace stress – control			
Type A and Type B behaviour			
Hardiness			
Stress inoculation therapy			
Research studies related to … • **6 marks' worth of description** • **6 marks' worth of evaluation (including the issues of reliability, validity and ethics)**			
The body's response to stress			
The relationship between the immune system and illness			
Stress-related illnesses			
Life changes			
Daily hassles			
Workplace stress – workload			
Workplace stress – control			
Personality factors – Type A			
Personality factors – Type B			
Personality factors – hardiness			
Psychological methods of stress management			
Biological methods of stress management			
Factors that affect … • **6 marks' worth of material**			
Stress			
Workplace stress			
Explanations/theories • **6 marks' worth of description** • **6 marks' worth of evaluation (strengths/limitations)**			
The body's response to stress			
Pituitary-adrenal system			
Sympathomedullary pathway			
Stress-related illness and the immune system			
Applications of stress research • **6 marks' worth of material** • **6 marks' worth of evaluation (strengths/limitations)**			
Two psychological methods of stress management (stress inoculation therapy plus one other)			
Two biological methods of stress management (two types of drugs)			

Cognitive psychology: Memory	>	Stress as a bodily response	>	The body's response to stress
Developmental psychology: Early social development	>	Stress in everyday life	>	Stress-related illness
Research methods	>		>	Life changes
Biological psychology: Stress	>			Daily hassles
Social psychology: Social influence	>			Workplace stress
Individual differences: Psychotherapy (abnormality)	>			Personality factors and stress

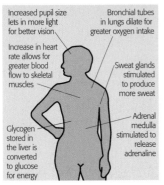

Increased pupil size lets in more light for better vision

Bronchial tubes in lungs dilate for greater oxygen intake

Increase in heart rate allows for greater blood flow to skeletal muscles

Sweat glands stimulated to produce more sweat

Adrenal medulla stimulated to release adrenaline

Glycogen stored in the liver is converted to glucose for energy

▲ *The sympathomedullary pathway (SNS activation)*

KEY TERMS

Fight or flight
- A term meaning an animal is energised to either fight or run away in response to a sudden (acute) stressor.

Pituitary-adrenal system
- Stress response involving the pituitary gland and **adrenal cortex**.
- Helps the body cope with chronic stressors.

Stress
- When the perceived demands of a situation are greater than the perceived ability to cope.

Sympathomedullary pathway
- A stress response, involving the **SNS** and **adrenal medulla**, which helps the body prepare for fight or flight.

▼ *The pituitary-adrenal system*

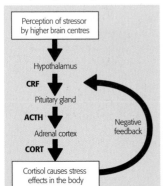

Perception of stressor by higher brain centres

Hypothalamus

CRF

Pituitary gland

ACTH

Adrenal cortex

CORT

Negative feedback

Cortisol causes stress effects in the body

The body's response to stress

The sympathomedullary pathway

The autonomic nervous system (ANS) – Immediate (acute) stressors activate the **sympathetic branch** of the ANS. The **sympathetic nervous system (SNS)** prepares the body for **fight or flight**, the rapid action necessary when an animal is under threat. This is achieved by the release of **noradrenaline**, which activates internal body organs associated with fight or flight.

SNS induced changes include an increase in heart rate and blood pressure, increased pupil size and metabolic changes, such as the mobilisation of fat and glucose in the bloodstream.

The adrenal medulla – A second part of this response to stress involves the adrenal glands, especially the **adrenal medulla**. Neurons of the SNS travel to the medulla, causing it to release **adrenaline** into the bloodstream. Adrenaline boosts the supply of oxygen and glucose to the brain and suppresses non-emergency bodily processes, such as digestion. Once the stressor has passed, the parasympathetic branch of the ANS slows the heartbeat down again and reduces blood pressure, restoring the body to its normal resting state.

The pituitary-adrenal system

The hypothalamus – This response is activated under conditions of chronic (ongoing) stress (see diagram below left). When such stressors are perceived by higher centres in the brain, a message is sent to the **hypothalamus**. Activation of this area leads to the production of **corticotrophin-releasing factor (CRF)**, which is released into the bloodstream.

The pituitary gland – On arrival at the **pituitary gland**, CRF causes it to release **adrenocorticotrophic hormone (ACTH)**. This is transported via the bloodstream to the adrenal glands, specifically the **adrenal cortex**.

The adrenal cortex – Once activated, the adrenal cortex releases the hormone **cortisol**, which has several effects throughout the body. Some are positive (e.g. lower sensitivity to pain), while some are negative (such as a lowered immune response). Prolonged release of ACTH by the pituitary causes the adrenal cortex to increase in size to produce more cortisol.

Evaluation: Consequences of the stress response

Cardiovascular problems – If stress responses are repeatedly activated, the heart and blood vessels begin to suffer from abnormal wear and tear. Increased blood pressure associated with SNS activation can lead to physical damage in the lining of blood vessels and increases the likelihood of heart disease.

Immunosuppression – Too much cortisol suppresses the **immune system**, shutting down the process that fights infection. Under normal conditions, a feedback system triggered by high cortisol levels causes a reduction in CRF and ACTH levels, thus bringing cortisol levels back to normal. This feedback system may break down under conditions of prolonged stress.

Individual differences – Whereas males tend to have a **fight or flight** response, females have a **tend and befriend** response, regulated by the hormone oxytocin.

⟳ PUTTING IT ALL TOGETHER

The stressors we typically face today are different from those faced by early humans. Therefore, the stress responses described above may not be universally adaptive under conditions of stress, and may actually be **maladaptive**.

Cognitive psychology: Memory		Stress as a bodily response	>	The body's response to stress
Developmental psychology: Early social development	>	Stress in everyday life	>	Stress-related illness
Research methods	>		>	Life changes
Biological psychology: Stress	>			Daily hassles
Social psychology: Social influence	>			Workplace stress
Individual differences: Psychotherapy (abnormality)				Personality factors and stress

Immune system
- Designed to defend the body against **antigens** (bacteria, viruses, toxins, etc.) that would otherwise invade it.
- White blood cells (**leucocytes**) identify and eliminate foreign bodies (antigens).
- The **sympathomedullary pathway** has a direct effect on the immune system – the **ANS** sends nerves directly into the tissues that form and store cells of the immune system.
- The **pituitary-adrenal system** increases levels of circulating **cortisol**, with too much cortisol suppressing the immune system.

Stress-related illness

Cardiovascular disorders

Stress can lead to **cardiovascular disorders** (disorders of the heart and circulatory system).

- **SNS** activation leads to constriction of blood vessels and a rise in blood pressure and heart rate.
- An increase in heart rate may wear away the lining of blood vessels.
- Stress leads to increased glucose levels in the bloodstream, which may block blood vessels (**atheroschlerosis**).

The role of anger – Some people respond to stress with greater feelings of anger. **Williams** asked 13,000 people to complete an anger **questionnaire**. Six years later their health was checked. Those highest on the anger scale were far more likely to have had a heart attack.

Evaluation

Research support – Orth-Gomér et al. found increase in heart attacks as a result of marital conflict.

Diathesis-stress – Stress may not have a direct impact on illness but may trigger an existing vulnerability to an illness such as depression.

PUTTING IT ALL TOGETHER

The immune system can fail us by being *under-vigilant*, letting infections enter the body, or *over-vigilant*, so that it is the immune system itself that causes illness. Stress might be associated with both these types of immune dysfunction.

Stress-related illness and the immune system

keySTUDY   Kiecolt-Glaser *et al.* (1984)

How? Natural experiment with medical students. The researchers assessed immune system functioning one month before an exam and then during the examination period itself.

Showed? Immune system activity was significantly reduced from a blood sample taken *during* the examination period compared to one taken one month *before*. This suggests that short-term stressors reduce the efficiency of immune system functioning.

Other research

Kiecolt-Glaser *et al.* studied the effects of unhappy relationships on **immune system** functioning. They found that blister wounds on the arms of couples who showed high levels of hostile behaviour during interactions healed at 60% of the rate of those couples who showed low levels of hostility.

Malarkey *et al.* found that marital conflict produced significant changes in adrenaline and noradrenaline levels, which could lead to poorer immune system functioning.

Evaluation

Research support – Segerstrom and Miller conducted a **meta-analysis** of 293 studies and found that short-term acute stressors could actually boost the immune system, prompting it to prepare itself for infections or injuries. Long-term chronic stressors however, led to suppression of the immune system.

Stress can enhance the immune system – Short-term stress can increase levels of sIgA, which helps protect against infection (Evans *et al.*).

Not a simple relationship – There are various reasons why it is difficult to establish a causal relationship between stress and the immune system (**Lazarus**).

1. Health is affected by many different factors (genetics, lifestyle, etc.) therefore there is little variance left to be accounted for by stress.

2. Health is fairly stable and slow to change, therefore it is difficult to demonstrate that exposure to particular stressors has caused a change in health.

3. To demonstrate exposure to stress and health changes over the long term is impractical, therefore researchers have concentrated on the impact of relatively short-term stressors.

Individual differences – Women show more adverse immunological changes in the way they react to chronic stressors such as marital conflict (**Kiecolt-Glaser *et al.***).

As people age, stress has a greater effect on immune system functioning, making it harder for the body to regulate itself (**Segerstrom and Miller**).

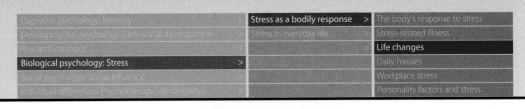

Cognitive psychology: Memory		Stress as a bodily response >	The body's response to stress
Developmental psychology: Early social development		Stress in everyday life	Stress-related illness
Research methods			Life changes
Biological psychology: Stress	>		Daily hassles
Social psychology: Social influence			Workplace stress
Individual differences: Psychotherapy (abnormality)			Personality factors and stress

Life changes
- Events (e.g. divorce or bereavement) that require a significant adjustment in a person's life.
- A significant source of **stress**.

Social Readjustment Rating Scale (SRRS)
- Developed by **Holmes and Rahe** to be able to test the idea that life changes are related to stress-related illnesses, such as **anxiety** and **depression**.
- The SRRS is based on 43 life events taken from an analysis of over 5000 patient records.
- Marriage is given a 'readjustment' score (life change unit, LCU) of 50.
- Events requiring more readjustment have a LCU higher than 50 and those requiring less have a LCU lower than 50.
- Highest LCU for a life event was death of a spouse (LCU of 100).

Validity and reliability of research findings

Validity – There are concerns over the accuracy of people's memories for life events. People who are unwell may feel a need to provide an explanation for their illness and so are more likely to report stressful events that might have caused it.

Reliability – There are also issues over the consistency of retrospective reports, with **Rahe** finding that **test-retest reliability** varies depending on the time interval between testing.

Life changes as stressors

keySTUDY Rahe *et al.* (1970)

How? Correlation using the SRE **questionnaire** (a military version of the **SRRS**) given to 2664 men aboard three US Navy ships. This measured the life events experienced over the previous six months. During their six-month tour of duty a record was kept of any illness.

Showed? They found a small but significant positive correlation between the men's **life change units** (LCU) over the previous six months and their illness over the same period. As there are both positive and negative events in the SRRS, this appears to indicate that it is not whether a change is considered negative that is important, but the amount of energy required in order to deal with the event that creates stress, and potentially illness.

Other research

Michael and Ben-Zur conducted a **natural experiment**. They studied men and women, half recently divorced and half recently widowed. For the bereaved group, levels of life satisfaction were greater *before* and lower *after* bereavement. For the divorced group this was the other way around, with higher levels of life satisfaction after the divorce than before.

Why was this the case? One possibility is that the divorced group were better able to turn this life change into a positive experience than a negative experience. This was harder for the bereaved group, therefore the negative impact of bereavement was more obvious in this group.

Evaluation

A spurious relationship – Most studies have yielded only correlational data, failing to demonstrate a *causal* relationship between life events and stress-related illness. It is possible that a third variable affects both.

Individual differences – There are huge individual differences in the impact of life events such as pregnancy, retirement and even relatively minor events such as Christmas or an annual holiday. Because the impact of these events varies from person to person it becomes hard to predict illness from SRRS scores alone.

Life changes and daily hassles – Major life changes are relatively rare in most people's lives, so relatively minor **daily hassles** are more likely to be a significant source of stress. **DeLongis *et al.*** found a significant relationship between health and daily hassles but not for life events.

Positive and negative events – Research using the SRRS appears to indicate that *any* life-changing event has the potential to damage health because it requires significant readjustment. Some critics argue that only undesired, unscheduled and uncontrolled changes tend to be *really* harmful.

Real-world application – Experience of life events such as financial troubles, physical illness and unemployment have been found to predict the likelihood of suicide (**Heikkinen and Lönnqvist**).

PUTTING IT ALL TOGETHER

Events such as the death of a loved one, divorce or a son/daughter leaving home are referred to as *critical* life events because they require a major transition in our lives. As such they can be a major source of stress. However, what might be profoundly stressful for one person, may be a blessed relief for another. Similarly, some life events, such as the death of a much loved pet, can be extremely stressful for some people. As a result, it is difficult to gauge the stressful impact of specific life events as stressors.

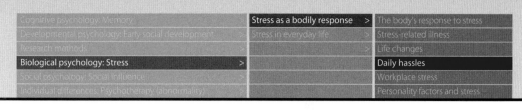

		Stress as a bodily response >	The body's response to stress
Cognitive psychology: Memory		Stress in everyday life >	Stress-related illness
Developmental psychology: Early social development >		>	Life changes
Research methods			Daily hassles
Biological psychology: Stress	>		Workplace stress
Social psychology: Social Influence			Personality factors and stress
Individual differences: Psychotherapy (abnormality)			

KEY TERMS

Daily hassles

- Hassles are those frustrating, irritating everyday experiences that occur regularly in our work, home and personal life.

- For most of us, our life stressors are not major **life changes** like divorce, redundancy or the death of a loved one, but the relatively minor annoyances that affect us more regularly and accumulate over time.

Daily uplifts

- Uplifts are the minor positive experiences of everyday life that often counter the negative effects of daily hassles.

- They include receiving a compliment at work or feeling good about our appearance.

↻ PUTTING IT ALL TOGETHER

Daily hassles are comparable to, if not greater than, life changes as a significant source of stress. However, the greater negative influence of daily hassles may be due, in part, to the reduced social support received from others, who may be more likely to lend their support when we experience important life changes, but not when we experience daily hassles.

Daily hassles as stressors

🔵 keySTUDY Bouteyre *et al.* (2007)

How? Correlational analysis of the relationship between **daily hassles** and mental health in students undergoing the initial transition from school to university. Students completed a hassles questionnaire and a **depression** inventory.

Showed? The researchers found that over 40% of the new students suffered from depressive symptoms and there was a positive correlation between scores on the hassles scale and the incidence of depressive symptoms.

⬡ Research evidence

Gervais asked nurses to keep diaries for a month, recording all the daily hassles and uplifts while at work. After a month, it was clear that daily hassles increased job strain and deceased job performance. However, **daily uplifts** appeared to counteract the stressful impact of these hassles as well as improving job performance.

Flett *et al.* found that major life events differ from daily hassles in the extent that individuals seek and receive social support. Negative effect of daily hassles may, in part, be due to reduced level of social support from others.

⬡ Evaluation

Memory problems – Most research on daily hassles has asked participants to assess the impact of hassles experienced over the previous month. The accuracy of such memories tends to vary according to the time interval involved. More recently, researchers have started to overcome this problem using a **diary method** where stressors and feelings are recorded daily.

Correlations don't show causal relationships – Even when memories *are* reliable, the data they produce are only correlational. This means that we can't draw causal relationships between daily hassles and our physical and psychological wellbeing. However, correlations do suggest that hassles have the *potential* to have adverse effects on our wellbeing, therefore we would be wise to take them seriously.

Real-world application – Research in this area gives us an insight into understanding road rage. **Gulian *et al.*** found that participants who reported a difficult day at work tended to report higher levels of stress on their drive home. When unresolved hassles from the day (e.g. arguments with fellow workers or job-related frustration) were carried forward, events such as the behaviour of other road users were more likely to be interpreted negatively by the stressed driver.

Pets as daily hassles – Miller *et al.* found gender differences in the impact of pets on an individual's life. For females, pets were commonly associated with uplifts (e.g. leisure), but for males they were more likely to be associated with hassles (e.g. cost of upkeep).

Explaining daily hassles

- **The accumulation effect** – There is an accumulation of minor daily stressors which creates persistent irritations, frustrations and overloads. This then results in more serious stress reactions, such as anxiety and depression.

- **The amplification effect** – Chronic stress caused by negative life events may deplete a person's resources, making them more vulnerable to the influence of daily hassles.

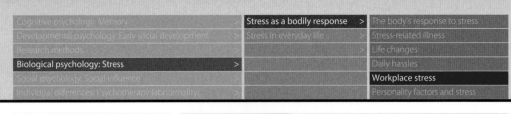

Cognitive psychology: Memory	Stress as a bodily response >	The body's response to stress
Developmental psychology: Early social development	Stress in everyday life >	Stress-related illness
Research methods		Life changes
Biological psychology: Stress		Daily hassles
Social psychology: Social influence		**Workplace stress**
Individual differences: Psychotherapy (abnormality)		Personality factors and stress

KEY TERMS

Cardiovascular disorder

- Disorders of the heart or circulatory system, including hypertension (high blood pressure) and heart disease.

Control

- The degree to which workers perceive that they have control over important aspects of their work, such as deadlines, procedures, etc.

Workload

- The demands of a person's work role.
- This can be stressful because it is repetitive, high intensity, monotonous or high volume.

Workplace stressors

- Aspects of our working environment that we experience as stressful, and which cause a stress reaction in our body.

Workplace stress

keySTUDY Marmot *et al.* (1997)

How? Longitudinal study. Over 7000 civil servants were asked to complete a **questionnaire** on workload, job **control** and the amount of social support they received from others. The researchers also checked for signs of **cardiovascular disorder**. Five years later, the participants were reassessed to see if their health status had changed.

Showed? The study produced two key results:

- **Workload** – **Marmot *et al.*** found no link between high workload and stress-related illness, suggesting that workload was not a significant factor in the development of stress-related illness. However, other studies (e.g. **Johansson *et al.*)** have found that performing repetitive jobs that require high levels of attention and responsibility were related to stress-related illness.

- **Control** – Those civil servants who initially reported low levels of job control were more likely to have developed heart disease than those who reported high levels of job control. This association was independent of employment grade or other risk factors such as smoking or physical activity. The critical risk factor for the development of heart disease was the level of control.

Evaluation

Individual differences – **Schaubroeck *et al.*** found that workers respond differently to lack of control. Some people are less stressed by having no control or responsibility and show better **immune responses** in such situations.

Work underload – Can be as stressful as work overload. **Shultz *et al.*** in a study across 15 European countries found that although employees reporting work overload were the most stressed, those reporting work underload also reported significant levels of stress.

Workplace stress and mental health – Although workplace stress may not directly cause mental health problems such as depression, when combined with other problems (such as personal problems) it can make depression more likely to occur.

The evolution of work and work stressors – The nature of the working environment is constantly changing with the advent of new technology and new working practices (including an increase in 'virtual' offices and a blurring of the home–work environment). This means that our current knowledge of workplace stressors rapidly becomes out of date. Consequently, psychological research may inevitably lag behind actual work practices.

Validity – Many of the studies of workplace stressors have made use of **questionnaires**. However, traditional questionnaires may distort the importance of some items that are no longer important (see point above), while ignoring others that have become a significant source of stress for most people. **Keenan and Newton** used interviews in a study of engineers and found that many of the significant stressors mentioned in this study (such as time-wasting job demands) are not included in questionnaires. They conclude that interviews are a more valid way of assessing the impact of workplace stressors than traditional questionnaires.

PUTTING IT ALL TOGETHER

There are many aspects of the working environment that are commonly reported as being 'stressful'. Each of the types of stressor described on this page has the *potential* to cause a stress reaction, and thus affect physical and psychological health. Whether they do have this effect or not depends on many other factors including an individual's ability to cope and the available social support.

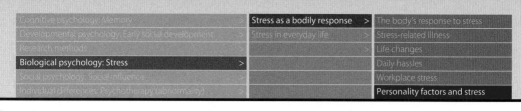

Cognitive psychology: Memory		Stress as a bodily response	>	The body's response to stress
Developmental psychology: Early social development	>	Stress in everyday life	>	Stress-related illness
Research methods			>	Life changes
Biological psychology: Stress	>			Daily hassles
Social psychology: Social influence	>			Workplace stress
Individual differences: Psychotherapy (abnormality)	>			Personality factors and stress

Type A and Type B personalities

Friedman and Rosenman described the **Type A personality** as possessing three major characteristics:

- Competitiveness and achievement striving.
- Impatience and time urgency.
- Hostility and aggressiveness.

These characteristics are believed to lead to raised blood pressure and an increase in levels of stress **hormones**, both of which are linked to ill health, particularly the development of **coronary heart disease** (CHD).

Type B behaviours, by contrast (e.g. relaxed and easygoing), decrease risk of stress-related illness.

keySTUDY Friedman and Rosenman (1960)

How? A **natural experiment** and **structured interview**, used to assess the personality of 3000 men between the ages of 39 and 59 (The Western Collaborative Group Study). The questions also assessed the way the men responded to everyday pressures. Participants were classed as Type A or B.

Western Collaborative Group Study

	Type A (%)	Type B (%)
Heart attacks	12.8	6.0
Recurring heart attacks	2.6	0.8
Fatal heart attacks	2.7	1.1

Showed? Eight years later, twice as many (12%) of those who had Type A personalities had died of cardiovascular problems than those who were classified as Type B. The Type A men also had higher blood pressure and higher levels of cholesterol.

Evaluation

The importance of hostility – Myrtek carried out a **meta-analysis** of 35 studies in this area and found an association between CHD and only one component of the Type A personality – hostility. There was no evidence of an association between CHD and other components of the Type A personality. This challenged the earlier conclusion that Type A behaviour was a significant risk factor for increased mortality from CHD.

Research support – Ragland and Brown carried out a follow-up study of Friedman and Rosenman's participants 22 years after the start of the study. They found 15% of the men had died of heart disease, but found no relationship between Type A personality and death from CHD, challenging the claim that Type A personality was a significant risk factor.

An outdated concept? Psychology's preoccupation with the Type A personality is, in part, a reflection of the importance of traditional masculinity in the 50s and 60s. As Type A men became aware of the health risks of their lifestyle, hardiness became more important as it emphasised the acquisition of positive health behaviours in men *and* women.

PUTTING IT ALL TOGETHER

There are important differences in the way that people react to stress. Research has established that some personality characteristics, such as those that lead to Type A behaviours, make us more vulnerable to the negative effects of stress. Others, such as those that lead to Type B behaviours, make us more resistant to those negative effects.

47

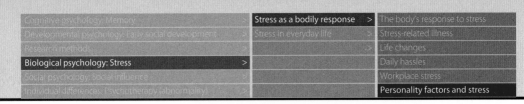

		Stress as a bodily response	>	The body's response to stress
Cognitive psychology: Memory	>	Stress in everyday life	>	Stress-related illness
Developmental psychology: Early social development	>		>	Life changes
Research methods				Daily hassles
Biological psychology: Stress	>			Workplace stress
Social psychology: Social influence				**Personality factors and stress**
Individual differences: Psychotherapy (abnormality)	>			

KEY TERMS

Hardy personality
- A type of personality, which provides a defence against the negative effects of **stress**.
- A hardy personality is high in control, commitment and challenge.

Personal Views Survey
- A measure of 'hardiness'.
- Hardiness score is a composite of three subscales: commitment, control and challenge.

⟳ PUTTING IT ALL TOGETHER

Relative to less hardy individuals, hardy individuals are able to function better when they encounter very stressful environments. Hardiness researchers have discovered why some people exposed to stressful environments suffer while others appear to thrive. Hardy individuals are more likely to see themselves as being in control of their lives, to have a strong sense of purpose and see life's challenges as problems to be overcome rather than as threats to their wellbeing.

Personality factors: The hardy personality

Kobasa and Maddi claim that some people are more resistant to the harmful effects of stress because they have a '**hardy personality**' which consists of:

- **Control** – Hardy people see themselves as being in control of their lives rather than being controlled by external factors.
- **Commitment** – Hardy people are involved with the world around them and have a strong sense of purpose.
- **Challenge** – Life challenges are seen as problems to be overcome rather than stressors.

🏅 keySTUDY Kobasa (1979)

How? The stress scores of 800 business executives were determined using Holmes and Rahe's **SRRS** and hardiness was assessed using a hardiness test.

Showed? Kobasa found that 150 of the executives were experiencing high levels of stress. However, these individuals differed in their illness record over the same period. Those with low levels of illness were more likely to have scored high on all three characteristics of the hardy personality and vice versa.

⬡ Other research

Maddi et al. measured hardiness in employees of a company that was dramatically reducing its workforce over a period of one year. They found that two-thirds suffered stress-related illness over the year, but the other third thrived, showing evidence of the three components of the hardy personality.

Lifton et al. measured hardiness in students at five US universities to see whether it was associated with the ability to cope with the stresses associated with academic life. They found that students scoring low on hardiness were disproportionately more likely to drop out of university, and those scoring high were more likely to complete their degree.

⬡ Evaluation

Negative affectivity (NA) may be a simpler explanation. Individuals with high NA dwell more on their failures and on negative aspects of themselves and are more likely to report dissatisfaction and distress (Watson and Clark). This suggests that 'hardy' individuals are simply those who are low on NA.

Problems of measurement – Much of the research support for a link between hardiness and health has relied on data obtained through self-report questionnaires. More recent research has used the **Personal Views Survey**, which has addressed many of the problems associated with earlier questionnaires, such as long and awkward wording and negatively worded items.

Real-world application – The concept of hardiness has been used to explain why some soldiers remain healthy, even under the extreme stress of combat. During the 1990s Gulf War, soldiers with higher levels of hardiness were better able to cope with combat stress without developing stress-related illnesses such as post-traumatic stress disorder (PTSD) or depression (**Bartone**). This has led to elite military units screening for hardiness as part of their selection procedures.

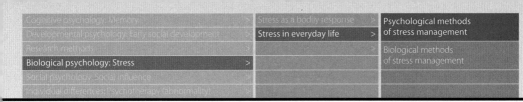

Cognitive psychology: Memory >	Stress as a bodily response >	Psychological methods of stress management
Developmental psychology: Early social development >	Stress in everyday life >	
Research methods >		> Biological methods of stress management
Biological psychology: Stress >		
Social psychology: Social influence >		
Individual differences: Psychotherapy (abnormality) >		

Psychological methods of stress management

Stress inoculation training

Meichenbaum believed that although we can't change the causes of **stress**, we can change the way we think about stressors and the way we react to them. People can be trained to 'inoculate' themselves against a stressor before it arises.

The three phases of stress inoculation training are:

- **Conceptualisation** – Clients are taught to think differently about stressors, i.e. as problems that can be solved.
- **Skills acquisition** – Coping skills are taught and rehearsed in real life.
- **Application** – Learned coping skills are applied in increasingly stressful situations.

Evaluation

Strengths
Effectiveness – Meichenbaum compared SIT with **systematic desensitisation** to deal with snake phobias. Both were effective *but* SIT helped to reduce fear associated with a second, as yet untreated phobia.

Reducing academic stress – Sheehy and Horan found that sessions of SIT reduced anxiety and stress among students over time, as well as improving their academic performance.

Preparation for future stressors – SIT gives the client the necessary skills so they are less adversely affected by stressors in the future.

Limitations
Time-consuming and requires high motivation – Although SIT has been criticised because of this, Meichenbaum has also demonstrated the effectiveness of relatively brief periods of training.

Unnecessarily complex – It is possible that effectiveness of SIT can still be achieved with just some of its elements. It may be equally effective to learn how to talk more positively and relax more.

Hardiness training

Kobasa and Maddi identified a personality type that was especially resistant to stress – the **hardy personality** (see page 48). They believed that people could be trained in hardiness, to help them manage stress better.

Hardiness training involves:

- **Focusing** – The client is taught to recognise the sources of stress and the physiological signs of stress.
- **Reliving stress encounters** – The client is given an insight into current coping strategies by reliving previous encounters and their response to them.
- **Self-improvement** – These insights can be used to move forward and learn new techniques, e.g. seeing stressors as challenges they can take control of rather than problems they must give in to.

Evaluation

Strengths
It works – Hardiness training has been shown to be effective in many different populations. For example, it has been shown to help at-risk students to deal with the stresses they face during their college life.

Real-world application – Hardiness training has been used to increase commitment to training in Olympic swimmers, by helping to control aspects of their daily lives that might interfere with their training schedules (**Fletcher**).

Limitation
Overcoming bad habits – Training must first address basic aspects of personality and learned habits of coping that are difficult to modify, therefore hardiness training cannot be seen as a rapid solution to stress management.

⟳ **PUTTING IT ALL TOGETHER**

These psychological approaches to stress management are an example of the problem-focused approach to coping. Individuals can change the way they think about problems in their life, or learn techniques that minimise the negative effects of stressful situations.

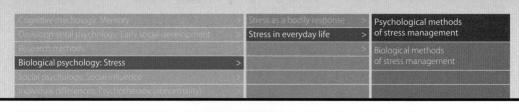

Cognitive psychology: Memory
Developmental psychology: Early social development
Research methods
Biological psychology: Stress >
Social psychology: Social influence >
Individual differences: Psychotherapy (abnormality) >

Stress as a bodily response >
Stress in everyday life >

Psychological methods of stress management

Biological methods of stress management

KEY TERMS

Benzodiazepines
- A group of drugs (e.g. *Librium* or *Valium*) used to treat anxiety and stress.
- Work by slowing down the activity of the **central nervous system**.

Beta-blockers
- Decrease **anxiety** by reducing the activity of **adrenaline/ noradrenaline**.
- These are released as part of the body's response to **stress**.

Placebo
- A drug or treatment that contains no active ingredient or therapeutic procedure.

Withdrawal symptoms
- Abnormal physical or psychological reactions to the abrupt discontinuation of a drug to which an individual has developed physical dependence.

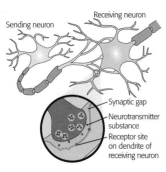

▲ *GABA is released from one neuron across the **synaptic gap** where it reacts with special receptors with the second receiving neuron. BZs are carried to special booster sites on these receptors, where they enhance the action of GABA.*

Receiving neuron
Sending neuron
Synaptic gap
Neurotransmitter substance
Receptor site on dendrite of receiving neuron

⟳ PUTTING IT ALL TOGETHER

Physiological methods of stress management are a form of emotion-focused coping because they focus on alleviating the emotions associated with the stressful situation rather than dealing with the situation itself.

Drug therapies

 Benzodiazepines (BZs)

Benzodiazepines are drugs that are used to treat the anxiety that is a consequence of stress. They do this by slowing down the activity of the central nervous system. How do they achieve this?

- **GABA** is a **neurotransmitter** that is the body's natural form of anxiety relief. GABA has a natural quietening effect on many of the **neurons** in the brain by indirectly making it harder for them to be stimulated by other neurotransmitters, slowing down their activity and making the person feel more relaxed.
- BZs enhance the action of GABA, making neurons in the brain even more resistant to excitation and making the person feel much calmer.

Beta-blockers (BBs)

Beta-blockers are drugs that reduce the activity of **adrenaline** and **noradrenaline** which are part of the **sympathomedullary** response to stress. Thus BBs can prevent some of the **cardiovascular** problems associated with chronic levels of stress. How do they achieve this?

- BBs reduce the activity of adrenaline and noradrenaline by binding to receptors on the cells of the heart and other parts of the body that are usually stimulated during arousal.
- By blocking these receptors, it is harder to stimulate these cells, so the heart beats slower and with less force, blood pressure falls, and so on. As a result, the person feels calmer and less anxious.

Evaluation

Research support – Kahn *et al.* conducted an **experiment** where a group of patients were given a drug and another group given a **placebo**. This enabled them to see if the success of a drug in reducing symptoms was attributable to its pharmacological properties or to something psychological. They followed 250 patients for eight weeks. BZs were significantly superior at reducing anxiety compared to placebo.

Strengths

Effectiveness, as illustrated by the research evidence above. Drugs have been shown to be effective in managing the effects of stress. **Hildalgo *et al.*** conducted a **meta-analysis** and found that BZs were more effective than other drugs for reducing anxiety.

Ease of use – Drug treatments require little effort from the patient compared to the significant investment in time and motivation required in the psychological methods discussed on the previous page.

Limitations

Addiction – Patients exhibit **withdrawal symptoms** when they stop taking BZs, indicating a psychological dependence, hence use of BZs is recommended to be limited to just four weeks.

Side effects – For BZs, these include increased aggressiveness and impairment of memory. Some studies have linked BBs to an increased risk of developing developmental diabetes.

Treating the symptoms rather than the problem – Effectiveness of drug treatments for stress and anxiety only lasts as long as the person takes the drug because the problem itself has not been addressed.

Chapter 5

Social psychology

Column 1: tick when you have produced brief notes.

Column 2: tick when you have a good grasp of this topic.

Column 3: tick during the final revision when you feel you have complete mastery of the topic.

Key terms • **3 marks' worth of material**	1	2	3
Conformity (majority influence)			
Internalisation			
Compliance			
Informational social influence			
Normative social influence			
Obedience			
Independent behaviour			
Locus of control			
Research studies related to … • **6 marks' worth of description** • **6 marks' worth of evaluation (including the issues of reliability, validity and ethics)**			
Conformity			
Obedience			
How people resist pressures to conform			
The role of social influence research in social change			
The role of minority influence in social change			
How people resist pressures to obey authority			
Influence of locus of control on independent behaviour			
Factors that affect … • **6 marks' worth of material**			
Conformity			
Obedience			
Independent behaviour (conformity)			
Independent behaviour (obedience)			
Independent behaviour (locus of control)			
Explanations/theories • **6 marks' worth of description** • **6 marks' worth of evaluation (both strengths and limitations)**			
Conformity			
Why people obey			
How people resist pressures to conform			
How people resist pressures to obey authority			
Influence of locus of control on independent behaviour			
Applications of social influence research • **6 marks' worth of material**			
Using social influence research to explain social change			
Using minority influence research to explain social change			

Cognitive psychology: Memory		Social influence	Conformity (majority influence)
Developmental psychology: Attachment		Social influence in everyday life	Explanations of why people conform
Research methods			Obedience
Biological psychology: Stress			Explanations of why people obey
Social psychology: Social influence			
Individual differences: Psychopathology (abnormality)			

KEY TERMS

Conformity

- A form of social influence.
- Results from exposure to the majority position.
- Leads to compliance with that position.
- The tendency for people to adopt the behaviour and attitudes of other members of their group.

⬡ Types of conformity

Kelman proposed different types of **conformity**:

Compliance – going along with others to gain their approval or avoid their disapproval. This is a result of social comparison, which enables an individual to adjust their behaviour to that of the group. There is no change in the person's underlying attitude, only their public behaviour.

Internalisation – going along with others because of an acceptance of their point of view. This is a result of an examination of the group's position, which may lead to *validation* of the person's own views, or acceptance of the group's views both in public and in private.

⟳ PUTTING IT ALL TOGETHER

Conforming to the views or behaviours of others may be a consequence of different psychological motivations (the need to be liked, the desire to be right). Results of the Asch study are primarily the result of the very human need to be accepted by others, therefore can be explained in terms of *compliance*, i.e. a change in public behaviour only.

Conformity (majority influence)

👤 keySTUDY Asch (1956)

How? Lab experiment, 123 male American undergraduates volunteered to take part in a test of their 'vision', although, unbeknown to these volunteers, all the other participants were **confederates** of the experimenter. Asch showed a series of lines to the participants seated around a table. Each, in turn, had to state out loud which of three comparison lines were the same length as a standard line. The real participant always answered last or second to last. On 12 of the 18 trials, the confederates were instructed to give the same incorrect answer.

Showed? On the 12 trials where confederates gave the same wrong answer, 36.8% of the responses given by the real participants were also incorrect (i.e. they conformed to the decision of the group). Only 25% of participants never conformed at all. Without confederates giving the wrong answers, participants were correct in their judgments 99% of the time.

Variations of this study showed that when the task was made more difficult, conformity increased, that the size of the majority was relatively important (provided it was over three) but that unanimity was vital otherwise conformity dropped away almost completely.

⬡ Evaluation

A child of its time? Perrin and Spencer had difficulty getting the same level of conformity in their 1980 replication, although they subsequently achieved this if they made the perceived costs of *not* conforming appear high. They concluded that Asch got the results he did because in 1956, America was in the grip of McCarthyism, a strong anti-Communist period when people were scared to be different from the majority.

Conformity or independence? An often overlooked fact is that on two-thirds of the trials where the majority gave the same *wrong* answer, the participant stuck to their original opinion. This suggests that rather than being overly conformist, human beings are able to display **independent behaviour** even in the face of an overwhelming majority.

Culture and conformity. A **meta-analysis** of studies of conformity across 17 countries by **Smith and Bond** established that **collectivist cultures** show significantly higher levels of conformity than **individualist cultures**. Levels of conformity also declined steadily since Asch's research, with the date of the study negatively correlated with the level of conformity found in the study. However, cultures are not homogenous in terms of individualist and collectivist values, so drawing **conclusions** based on differences *between* cultures is an oversimplification.

Gender differences in conformity

Eagly and Carli carried out a meta-analysis of studies and found that women are generally more compliant than men. However, they also found that male researchers were much more likely to find gender differences than female researchers, possibly because they used experimental materials that were more familiar to males than to females.

Unconvincing confederates – Asch's study could be criticised because the confederates used would have found it difficult to act convincingly in their role. A study by **Mori and Arai** overcame this problem by using polarizing filters, which altered what each participant actually saw (therefore not requiring confederates). They found levels of conformity similar to those obtained by Asch for women (although not for men) suggesting that Asch's confederates had acted convincingly in the original study.

Cognitive psychology: Memory		Social influence	Conformity (majority influence)
Developmental psychology: Attachment		Social influence in everyday life	Explanations of conformity
Research methods			Obedience
Biological psychology: Stress			Explanations of why people obey
Social psychology: Social influence			
Individual differences: Psychopathology (abnormality)			

KEY TERMS

Normative social influence
- The result of wanting to be liked and accepted by a group.
- This results in a decision to follow group norms.
- Tends to result in **compliance**.

Informational social influence
- The result of wanting to be right.
- Believing that the majority has the right answer.
- Conforming to their opinion.
- Tends to result in **internalisation**.

Explanations of conformity

Normative social influence

This happens when an individual acts in the same way as the majority without actually *accepting* their point of view. It is conformity in action alone, and is also known as **compliance**. Because humans are a social species, they have a strong desire to be accepted and a fear of rejection. This makes it difficult for them to deviate from the majority, because of the risk of rejection. This fear forms the basis of normative social influence.

Evaluation

Bullying – The power of normative social influence has been demonstrated in a study on bullying. **Garandeau and Cillessen** showed how children with a low level of friendship can be manipulated by a skilful bully so that victimising another child provides the group with a common goal. This puts pressure on group members to comply to maintain the friendship of the other members of the group.

Normative influence and smoking – Generally accepted that there is a strong correlation between people's normative beliefs and their behaviour. This was supported in a US study (**Linkenbach and Perkins**), which found that adolescents exposed to normative message that majority of age peers did not smoke were subsequently less likely to take up smoking.

Conservation behaviour – **Schultz *et al.*** found that hotel guests exposed to the normative message that 75% of guests reused their towels each day reduced their own need for daily fresh towels by 25%.

Informational social influence

In other cases, individuals may go along with the majority because they genuinely believe them to be right, i.e. they have more information than the individual has about that particular issue. This tends to result in the individual conforming in both behaviour *and* attitude (i.e. both public and private change), therefore is an example of **internalisation**.

Informational social influence is most likely when:
- The situation is ambiguous, i.e. the right course of action is not clear.
- The situation is a crisis, i.e. rapid action is required.
- We believe others to be experts, i.e. we believe that others are more likely to know what to do.

Evaluation

Political opinion – research has supported the important role that informational social influence plays in shaping opinion. For example, **Fein *et al.*** showed how judgments of candidate performance in US presidential debates could be influenced by knowledge of the reactions of the majority. Participants who saw on screen what they thought were the reactions of fellow participants during the debate shifted their judgment of the candidates' performance in the direction of what they thought was the majority opinion.

Development of social stereotypes – Importance of informational influence demonstrated in a study that showed that exposure to negative information about African Americans more likely to shape social stereotypes if represented as 'view of the majority' (**Wittenbrink and Henly**).

Mass psychogenic illness – **Jones *et al.*** used informational social influence to explain how illness symptoms can spread rapidly among members of a cohesive group even though there is no obvious physical cause.

⟳ **PUTTING IT ALL TOGETHER**

People conform for many reasons, ranging from complete acceptance of the majority viewpoint (i.e. internalisation), to 'going along' with the crowd (compliance). Two explanations are normative social influence, when we follow the crowd, and informational social influence, when we accept the majority viewpoint because it is most likely to be right.

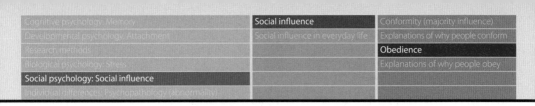

Cognitive psychology: Memory	Social influence	Conformity (majority influence)
Developmental psychology: Attachment	Social influence in everyday life	Explanations of why people conform
Research methods		Obedience
Biological psychology: Stress		Explanations of why people obey
Social psychology: Social influence		
Individual differences: Psychopathology (abnormality)		

KEY TERMS

Obedience to authority

- A type of social influence.
- Somebody acts in response to a direct order from a figure with perceived authority.
- There is also the implication that the person receiving the order is made to respond in a way that they would not have done without the order.

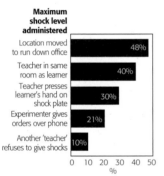

Maximum shock level administered

Location moved to run down office	48%
Teacher in same room as learner	40%
Teacher presses learner's hand on shock plate	30%
Experimenter gives orders over phone	21%
Another 'teacher' refuses to give shocks	10%

0 10 20 30 40 50
%

⟳ PUTTING IT ALL TOGETHER

In this form of social influence, the individual is faced with the choice of whether to comply with a direct order from a person with higher status or whether to defy the order. The ethics of Milgram's study have been questioned as has its validity as a representation of real-life obedience. Zimbardo claims that the reason why Milgram's research has attracted so much hostile criticism is because of *what* he discovered, not because of *how* he discovered it.

Obedience

🎓 keySTUDY Milgram (1963)

How? Lab experiment, varying different situational pressures to see which had the greatest effect on obedience.

- Forty male volunteers were told it was a study of how punishment affects learning.
- After drawing lots (which was rigged), the real participant was assigned the role of 'teacher'. The learner was a **confederate**.
- The teacher's job was to administrate a learning task and deliver 'electric shocks' to the learner (in another room) if he got a question wrong.
- The shocks began at 15 volts and increased in increments of 15 volts to a maximum of 450 volts.

Showed? All participants went to at least 300 volts, with only 12.5% stopping at that point. An astonishing 65% of the participants continued to the maximum 450 volts, showing high levels of obedience.

⬡ Milgram's variations

Milgram conducted variations to the original study (see graph on left) and found the following:

Proximity of the victim (e.g. they could be seen) decreased obedience, presumably because it removed the psychological **buffer** between action (giving shocks) and consequence. With the learner in the same room as the participant, obedience levels dropped to 40%. In the touch proximity condition, obedience levels dropped to 30%.

Proximity of authority figure made participants feel they were being monitored, so obedience levels were high. When the experimenter left the room and gave orders over the telephone, participants felt better able to defy, and obedience levels dropped to 21%.

Presence of allies – In the 'two peers rebel' study, two confederates shared the teacher's role with the real participant. When they refused to carry on, almost all participants also withdrew.

⬡ Evaluation

Ethics

- **Deception and lack of informed consent** – Participants were misled by being told the experiment was about the effects of punishment on learning rather than its true purpose (obedience). Consequently, participants were effectively denied the right to informed consent.
- **Protection from psychological harm – Baumrind** claimed that Milgram had placed his participants under great emotional strain, causing psychological damage that could not be justified. In his defence, Milgram argued that post-study interviews found no evidence of such harm.

Internal validity – Orne and Holland claim that people have learned to distrust experimenters in psychology because they know the real purpose of the experiment is likely to be disguised. Consequently, participants must have known they were not giving real shocks, particularly when the experimenter appeared completely unconcerned over the learner's cries of pain.

External validity – Mandel argued that Milgram's conclusions about the situational determinants of obedience in situations such as the Holocaust are not borne out by real-life events, and quotes **Browning**'s study of Reserve Police Battalion 101 at Josefow to support this assertion.

Cognitive psychology: Memory		Social influence	Conformity (majority influence)
Developmental psychology: Attachment		Social influence in everyday life	Explanations of why people conform
Research methods			Obedience
Biological psychology: Stress			**Explanations of obedience**
Social psychology: Social influence			
Individual differences: Psychopathology (abnormality)			

KEY TERMS

Agentic shift
- People may move from being in a state where they take personal responsibility for their actions (an **autonomous state**) to a state where they believe they are acting on behalf of an authority figure (an **agentic state**).

Monocausal emphasis
- Relying on just one causal factor when explaining an event.

Obedience alibi
- Reaching a conclusion that obedience had a key role in **Holocaust** events when such a conclusion is unjustified given an analysis of the historical record.

Explanations of obedience

Gradual commitment

In **Milgram's** study, participants have already committed themselves to giving lower level shocks, and therefore it is harder to resist the experimenter's requirement to give shocks at a higher level. As the transition from one shock level to another is very gradual (15 volt increments), it becomes even harder for participants to change their minds about continuing. This is an example of what psychologists call the 'foot in the door' approach, once someone signals their willingness to agree to a small request, their ability to refuse larger requests from the same source diminishes.

Agentic shift

Milgram argued that people shift back and forwards between an **autonomous state**, where they see themselves as responsible for their own actions, and an **agentic state**, where they see themselves as an agent for carrying out the instructions of another person. When they perceive themselves as receiving an order from someone in authority, they shift from the former to the latter.

The role of buffers

In Milgram's base-line study, the 'teacher' and 'learner' were in separate rooms, therefore, when the teacher delivered an electric shock they did not have to witness the consequences. **Buffers** such as physical distance therefore protect the individual from at least some of the distress they may otherwise experience when they carry out actions that harm another person.

Evaluation

Mandel claims that Milgram's explanation of obedience, particularly when applied to the Holocaust, is oversimplified and misleading.

Monocausal emphasis – Mandel suggests that by focusing solely on obedience as an explanation for the atrocities carried out in the Holocaust, Milgram ignored many other plausible explanations. Goldhagen argues that **anti-Semitism** was the primary motivation for these acts, and that Germans did not need the pressure of authority to allow them to discriminate against, and ultimately kill, Jews.

Agentic shift – It is inappropriate to draw parallels between Milgram's lab and Holocaust events. Holocaust perpetrators carried out their duties over years, yet Milgram's participants were involved for just half an hour. There is also a difference in their perception of harm-doing, with Holocaust perpetrators *knowing* they were causing harm, whereas Milgram's participants were assured there would be no permanent damage.

Consequences of an obedience alibi – By attributing Holocaust events to obedience, Mandel argues that:

- The suggestion that Holocaust perpetrators were 'just obeying orders' is distressing for all those whose lives were affected by the Holocaust.
- Such an explanation effectively exonerates war criminals of their crimes.

Real-world application – Insights from Milgram's research can help us understand some of the abusive behaviour of guards at the Abu Ghraib prison in Iraq. For example, in Milgram's study gradual commitment was one of the most important determinants of obedience. The prisoner abuses observed in Abu Ghraib were also gradual in nature, coupled with the presence of compliant peers and an apparently unconcerned authority figure.

⟲ **PUTTING IT ALL TOGETHER**

Milgram was able to demonstrate the power of the situation in shaping behaviour, with moral constraints such as conscience and compassion being sidelined when an individual is confronted with a powerful authority figure.

Cognitive psychology: Memory		Social influence	Independent behaviour	
Developmental psychology: Attachment		Social influence in everyday life	Understanding social change	
Research methods				
Biological psychology: Stress				
Social psychology: Social influence				
Individual differences: Psychopathology (abnormality)				

KEY TERMS

Locus of control

- An aspect of our personality.
- People differ in their causal beliefs.
- The outcomes of their actions are contingent on either:
  - what they are or what they do (**internal control**, **internals**); or
  - events outside their personal control (**external control**, **externals**).

Locus of control

- High **internals** perceive themselves as having a great deal of personal control over their behaviour, so take more responsibility for it.
- High **externals** perceive their behaviour as caused more by external influences, so take less responsibility for it.

Individuals high in internality are more likely to display independent behaviour, for example:

- High internals are active seekers of information and rely less on the opinions of others.
- High internals are better able to resist coercion from others.

Evaluation

Research evidence – People high in internality rely more on their own actions and exhibit greater initiative, which should make them more successful. **Linz and Semykina** collected data from over 2600 Russian employees. Although there was no relationship between earnings (a measure of success) and locus of control for men, there was for women. **Internals** were the highest wage earners.

Research evidence – a meta-analysis by **Twenge et al.** found that locus of control scores had become substantially more external in young people between 1960 and 2002. The increase in externality means that young people see many aspects of their lives as beyond their control.

Independent behaviour – Resisting social influence

Resisting conformity

The role of allies – **Asch** showed how the introduction of another person who went against the majority caused conformity rates to drop significantly, but why?

A fellow dissenter provides the individual with an assessment of reality, making them more confident in their own decision. Conformity levels dropped even when the dissenter gave a *wrong* answer. This suggests that it is breaking the group's consensus that is important in increasing resistance.

Evaluation

Moral considerations – People conform to a majority position even though they know the majority position is wrong. The costs of conforming in Asch's study are minor given the insignificance of the task, and the benefits are significant (not looking foolish). However, if the task involves a moral dimension (e.g. cheating), there is less evidence of conformity as the costs incurred are significantly greater.

Individual differences – **Griskevicius et al.** suggest gender differences in mate seeking behaviour, with women displaying more conformity (e.g. to norms of what men find attractive) whereas men display less conformity in their behaviour. This fits with an evolutionary explanation of male behaviour when seeking romantic partners. This 'difference to the norm' is a successful strategy because it offers something different to prospective partners.

Resisting obedience

Status – When **Milgram's** study was moved from the prestigious setting of Yale University to a downtown office, more participants felt able to resist the experimenter. This tells us that status of the authority figure is a key factor in obedience and its resistance.

Proximity – Resistance increased when the victim could be seen, or when other **confederates** were present. Being made aware of the effects of obedient actions and having social support makes it more likely that the individual will feel able to resist pressures to obey.

Evaluation

Moral considerations – **Kohlberg** interviewed participants who had obeyed the experimenter and those who had resisted. He found that those who based their decision on more advanced moral principles (e.g. the importance of justice over social order) were more defiant, whereas those who obeyed the experimenter completely tended to reason at a lower moral stage.

Individual differences – Milgram found that educational history and religion made a difference when it came to being able to resist the commands of the experimenter. Less-educated participants were less able to resist and Roman Catholics were also more likely to obey the experimenter than were Protestants.

PUTTING IT ALL TOGETHER

People are not simply at the mercy of situational factors, and may be able to resist their influence. Whether someone conforms, obeys or displays independent behaviour may be determined by the personal characteristics of the individual as well as what they are trying to achieve.

Cognitive psychology: Memory		
Developmental psychology: Attachment		
Research methods		
Biological psychology: Stress		
Social psychology: Social influence		
Individual differences: Psychopathology (abnormality)		

| Social influence | Independent behaviour |
| Social influence in everyday life | Understanding social change |

PUTTING IT ALL TOGETHER

The power that persuasive minorities have to bring about social change is their ability to organise, educate and mobilise support for their cause. Insights from research on minority influence help us to understand how the minority groups might achieve social change, and by analysis of historical examples, how they *have* achieved this.

Minority influence and social change

Based on the idea that, if an individual is exposed to a persuasive argument under certain conditions, they may change their views to match those of the minority, a process referred to as 'conversion' (**Moscovici**).

Conditions necessary for social change through minority influence

- **Drawing attention to an issue** – Being exposed to a minority viewpoint (which opposes that of the majority) creates a conflict, which the individual is motivated to reduce. Illustrated in the actions of *Fathers4Justice*, an organisation which attempts to draw attention to the issue of fathers' rights after divorce.

- **The role of conflict** – Means that we examine the minority position more deeply, which may then result in a move towards that position. For example, a conflict between the arguments of the animal rights movement and our present use of cosmetics produces a conflict, which might lead to **social change** in terms of reduced use of cosmetics tested on animals.

- **Consistency** – When minorities express their arguments consistently (with each other and over time), they are taken more seriously and are more likely to bring about social change. **Meta-analysis** of 97 studies by **Wood et al.** showed that minorities perceived as being consistent were particularly influential in changing the views of the majority.

- **The augmentation principle** states that if there are risks involved in putting forward a particular point of view (e.g. abuse or imprisonment), then those who express those views are taken more seriously by others. As a result, the impact of their position is strengthened, or 'augmented'. This was demonstrated in the struggles of the Polish trade union *Solidarity*, whose members suffered censorship and imprisonment, yet grew to over 10 million members and was ultimately responsible for the overthrow of the Communist government in Poland in 1989.

Evaluation through analysis of the suffragettes

Drawing attention to an issue – The **suffragettes** used a variety of educational, political and militant tactics to draw attention to the fact that women were denied the same political rights as men.

The role of conflict – The suffragettes advocated a different political voting arrangement to that already in place. This created a conflict in the minds of the majority, some of whom dismissed the suffragettes as troublemakers, but others moved toward the suffragette position.

Consistency – The suffragettes were consistent in expressing their position, regardless of the attitudes of those around them. Their fight for the vote continued for 15 years, even when some were imprisoned.

The augmentation principle – The fact that the suffragettes were willing to suffer to make their point, risking imprisonment or even death from hunger strike, meant that they were taken more seriously by the majority. This resulted in social change within the UK, when women were finally given the vote in 1918.

Further evaluation

Minority influence doesn't necessarily lead to social change – Minorities are not only lacking in social power but may also be seen as 'deviant' by the majority. Their influence may be more latent than real (i.e. creating the potential for change rather than leading directly to social change).

Real-world application – **Kruglanski** claims that social change through **terrorism** may be understood using the principles of social change. Terrorists show consistency in their actions and by showing willingness to die for their beliefs demonstrate a commitment to their cause (augmentation principle).

57

CHAPTER 6

Individual differences

Column 1: tick when you have produced brief notes.

Column 2: tick when you have a good grasp of this topic.

Column 3: tick during the final revision when you feel you have complete mastery of the topic.

Key terms • 3 marks' worth of material • Limitations associated with each definition	1	2	3
Deviation from social norms			
Failure to function adequately			
Deviation from ideal mental health			
Research studies related to … • **6 marks' worth of description** • **6 marks' worth of evaluation (including the issues of reliability, validity and ethics)**			
Drug therapy			
ECT			
Psychoanalysis			
Systematic desensitisation			
Cognitive Behavioural Therapy			
Explanations/theories • **6 marks' worth of description** • **6 marks' worth of evaluation (both strengths and limitations)**			
Deviation from social norms			
Failure to function adequately			
Deviation from ideal mental health			
Biological approach to psychopathology			
Psychological approach: Psychodynamic			
Psychological approach: Behavioural			
Psychological approach: Cognitive			
Drug therapy			
ECT			
Psychoanalysis			
Systematic desensitisation			
Cognitive Behavioural Therapy			

Cognitive psychology: Memory		Defining and explaining psychological abnormality	Definitions of abnormality
Developmental psychology: Attachment			The biological approach
Research methods		Treating abnormality	The psychodynamic approach
Biological psychology: Stress			The behavioural approach
Social psychology: Social influence			The cognitive approach
Individual differences: Psychopathology (abnormality)			

KEY TERMS

Cultural relativism
- The view that ideas of normal and abnormal behaviour differ from culture to culture.

Deviation from ideal mental health
- Abnormality is seen as deviating from an ideal of positive mental health.
- This includes a positive attitude toward the self and an accurate perception of reality.

Deviation from social norms
- Abnormal behaviour is a deviation from unwritten rules about how one 'ought' to behave.
- Violation of these rules is considered abnormal.

Failure to function adequately
- Mentally healthy people are judged as being able to operate within certain acceptable limits.
- If abnormal behaviour interferes with daily functioning, it may be considered abnormal.

PUTTING IT ALL TOGETHER

All these definitions have their problems, therefore the definition of abnormality inevitably remains a subjective judgment. Consequently, abnormality is usually determined by the presence of several of these characteristics at the same time rather than one alone.

Definitions of abnormality

Deviation from social norms

All societies have social norms – standards of acceptable behaviour such as politeness, appropriate sexual behaviour, etc. These are not formal laws but implicit (i.e. unwritten) rules concerning what people expect from the behaviour of others. People who behave in a socially deviant way (i.e. they display behaviour that breaks these unwritten rules) are considered anti-social or undesirable – therefore *abnormal* – by the rest of the group.

Limitations of the 'deviation from social norms' definition

Deviance is related to context and degree – Judgments of deviance are dependent on the *context* of a behaviour. Some behaviours are considered acceptable in one context but not in another. There is also no clear line between what is an abnormal deviation and what is harmless eccentricity.

Cultural relativism – Any attempt to define a behaviour as abnormal is futile without also considering the culture in which it occurs. What is considered a diagnosable disorder and therefore 'abnormal' in one culture may be considered acceptable and therefore 'normal' in another. This means there are no universal standards for labelling a behaviour as abnormal.

Failure to function adequately

From an individual's point of view, abnormality can be judged in terms of 'not being able to cope'. Feeling **depressed** does not become a problem for the individual until their depression begins to interfere with their ability to cope with day-to-day living. When this happens, people may label their own behaviour as abnormal and seek treatment.

Limitations of the 'failure to function adequately' definition

Adaptive or maladaptive? – Some behaviours that *appear* dysfunctional and abnormal may actually be adaptive for the individual. For example, depression may lead to welcome extra attention for the individual, which helps them deal with the stressor that led to the depression in the first place.

Cultural relativism – Definitions of adequate functioning are also related to cultural ideals of how one's life should be lived. This means that the 'failure to function adequately' criterion of abnormality is likely to result in different diagnoses when applied to people from different cultures because the standard of one culture is being used to measure another.

Deviation from ideal mental health

Jahoda identified six characteristics of ideal mental health, such as:
- *Self-attitudes* – positive self-esteem and a strong sense of identity.
- *Integration* – being able to deal with stressful events.
- *Accurate perception of reality.*

This definition proposes that the *absence* of these criteria indicates abnormality and a potential mental disorder.

Limitations of the 'deviation from ideal mental health' definition

Who can achieve all these criteria? – According to this definition, all of us are abnormal to some degree, as it is unusual to find people that satisfy all the criteria all of the time.

Cultural relativism – Most of these criteria are culture-bound. If we apply them to non-Western cultures, we will probably find a higher incidence of abnormality. Some criteria, such as **self-actualisation**, are relevant to members of **individualist cultures** but not to members of **collectivist cultures**.

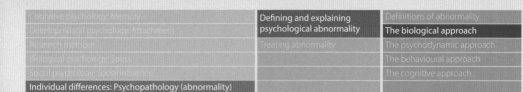

Cognitive psychology: Memory	Defining and explaining psychological abnormality	Definitions of abnormality
Developmental psychology: Attachment		The biological approach
Research methods	Treating abnormality	The psychodynamic approach
Biological psychology: Stress		The behavioural approach
Social psychology: Social influence		The cognitive approach

Individual differences: Psychopathology (abnormality)

KEY TERMS

Biological approach to psychopathology
- Explains behaviour in terms of physiological and/or genetic causes.
- A mental disorder represents the consequences of a malfunction of biological processes.

Concordance rates
- A measure of similarity between two individuals or sets of individuals on a given trait.
- Usually expressed as a percentage.

Diathesis-stress model
- In the case of certain disorders, individuals inherit a vulnerability (the diathesis) for the disorder.
- The disorder only develops if such individuals are exposed to difficult environmental conditions (**stress**).
- The greater the underlying vulnerability, the less stress is needed to trigger the disorder.

Genetic inheritance
- The reception of genetically coded traits as a result of transmission from parent to offspring.

Neuroanatomy
- The branch of anatomy that deals with the structure of the brain and other parts of the nervous system.

Neurochemistry
- The action of chemicals (e.g. **neurotransmitters**) in the brain and the drugs that influence neural activity.

The biological approach to psychopathology

Abnormality is caused by physical factors – The **biological approach to psychopathology** assumes that, like physical disorders, mental disorders are related to change, illness or dysfunction in the body.

Genetic inheritance – Abnormalities in brain anatomy (**neuroanatomy**) or brain chemistry (**neurochemistry**) are a product of genetic inheritance and so are passed from parent to child. **Concordance rates** are a way of measuring the extent to which two individuals are alike in terms of a specific trait (such as **schizophrenia**). If identical twins display high concordance rates for a mental disorder, such as schizophrenia, then it suggests a significant genetic influence is at work.

Neuroanatomy and neurochemistry – Abnormalities in the structure of the brain may determine abnormality. For example, some schizophrenics have enlarged spaces (ventricles) in their brains, indicating shrinkage of the brain tissue around the ventricles. Altered brain chemistry can lead to abnormal behaviour, e.g. low levels of **serotonin** have been found in the brains of individuals suffering from **depression**.

Viral infection – Some disorders may be explained in terms of exposure to viruses in the womb. Research has found that mothers of some schizophrenics have contracted a strain of the influenza virus during pregnancy. The virus is thought to enter the unborn child's brain, remaining dormant until puberty.

Limitations of the biological approach

Humane or inhumane? The emergence of a biological approach to abnormality meant that mental illness could be treated. However, **Szasz** suggested that the concept of 'mental illness' was invented merely to control (through the use of drugs or hospitalisation) those individuals who society could not accept as they are. He argued that unlike physical illnesses, most mental disorders did not have a physical basis, therefore could not be treated in the same way.

Inconclusive evidence – If mental disorders are caused by genetic factors alone, then concordance rates would be 100% for that mental disorder. In twin studies of schizophrenia, the concordance is only about 50%, suggesting that environmental influences are equally important. It is possible that what is inherited is a vulnerability to the disorder (a diathesis), which only develops under certain stressful conditions (**diathesis-stress model**).

Cause or effect? There isn't a simple cause and effect relationship between biological influences and mental disorders. Research has shown that some schizophrenics have enlarged ventricles, but it is not clear whether these are the cause of schizophrenic symptoms or a consequence of them (e.g. the result of taking medication to treat schizophrenia).

PUTTING IT ALL TOGETHER

One of the advantages of this approach is that its ideas can be tested scientifically. For example, biochemical explanations can be tested using experiments that alter levels of a specific neurotransmitter in the brain. If symptoms improve (compared to those in a **placebo** condition), this supports the influence of biochemical factors.

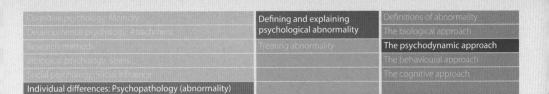

Cognitive psychology: Memory		Defining and explaining psychological abnormality	Definitions of abnormality
Developmental psychology: Attachment			The biological approach
Research methods		Treating abnormality	**The psychodynamic approach**
Biological psychology: Stress			The behavioural approach
Social psychology: Social Influence			The cognitive approach
Individual differences: Psychopathology (abnormality)			

KEY TERMS

Ego
- The conscious, rational part of a personality.
- Develops because a young child must deal with the constraints of reality and so is governed by the **reality principle**.

Ego defences
- Unconscious methods, such as repression and projection, which help protect an individual from feelings of anxiety.

Id
- The irrational, primitive part of a personality.
- Demands immediate satisfaction and is ruled by the **pleasure principle**.

Oedipal conflict
- Incestuous feelings that a young boy develops for his mother, coupled with rivalry with his father for her affections, leading to castration anxiety.
- Resolution of this conflict leads to the development of the superego.

Psychodynamic approach to psychopathology
- Any approach that emphasises the dynamics of behaviour.
- In other words, what *drives* us to behave in particular ways.

Superego
- Develops between the ages of 3 and 6.
- Embodies our conscience and sense of right and wrong, as well as notions of the ideal self.

The psychodynamic approach to psychopathology

Mental disorders have psychological not physical causes – Freud's **psychodynamic approach to psychopathology** believed that mental illnesses were not physical in origin but were the result of unresolved childhood conflicts.

Conflicts between the **id**, **ego** and **superego** create anxiety. This can be relieved by the use of **ego defences** such as **repression** (moving unpleasant thoughts into the unconscious), **projection** (blaming someone else for something a child cannot deal with) and **regression** (behaving like a child when faced with a difficult situation). These unconscious defences can be the cause of disturbed behaviour if they are overused.

Early experiences cause mental disorder – In childhood, the ego is not mature enough to deal with traumas such as the loss of a parent, so this may lead to repression of any associated emotions. Later in life, further losses may cause the individual to re-experience this earlier loss, leading to **depression**.

Unconscious motivations and mental disorder – The unconscious mind exerts a powerful effect on behaviour through the influence of previously repressed emotions or trauma. This frequently leads to distress, as the individual does not understand why they are acting in that particular way. The underlying problem cannot be controlled until it is brought into conscious awareness.

Rep
Pr
Reg.

Limitations of the psychodynamic approach

Abstract concepts – Concepts such as the id, ego and superego are abstract and therefore difficult to define and to demonstrate through research. Because conflicts between these three aspects of the personality operate at a primarily unconscious level, there is no way to know for certain that they are operating. As a result, psychodynamic explanations of psychopathology have received little empirical (i.e. research) support.

Lack of research support – The theory is difficult to prove or disprove using scientific methodology, therefore much of the support is from **case studies**. However, **Fisher and Greenberg** reviewed over 2500 **experimental** studies of Freudian hypotheses, and discovered that many of Freud's major claims received experimental support. A problem for research into psychoanalysis is that positive results are taken as supporting the hypothesis, but negative results are often also used as support because, it can be argued that, defence mechanisms disguise the real underlying conflict.

Sexism – Freud's theory is sexually unbalanced (e.g. his emphasis on the **Oedipal conflict** in boys which, he claimed, led to superior moral development). However, this is not surprising given that Freud himself was male, and at the time he was writing, the cultural bias meant that women were considered less significant than men. Nonetheless, this does limit the relevance of this approach to understanding the development of mental disorders in women.

PUTTING IT ALL TOGETHER

Psychodynamic theorists believe that an individual's abnormal behaviour is determined by underlying psychological conflicts of which they are largely unaware (i.e. they are the product of unconscious forces). The best-known psychodynamic theorist is Freud. He believed that unconscious forces determined all normal *and* abnormal behaviour.

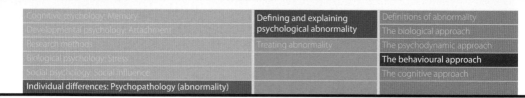

Cognitive psychology: Memory		Defining and explaining psychological abnormality	Definitions of abnormality
Developmental psychology: Attachment			The biological approach
Research methods		Treating abnormality	The psychodynamic approach
Biological psychology: Stress			**The behavioural approach**
Social psychology: Social influence			The cognitive approach
Individual differences: Psychopathology (abnormality)			

KEY TERMS

Behavioural approach to psychopathology

- Behaviourists believe that normal *and* abnormal behaviours are acquired as a result of experiences that we have in life.
- Abnormal behaviours are learned through the processes of **classical** and **operant conditioning** and **social learning**.

Maladaptive behaviour

- Any behaviour that inhibits a person's ability to cope with, or adjust to, particular situations.

Social learning theory

- The assumption that people learn through indirect as well as direct rewards by observing the behaviour of models (**observational learning**).
- And then imitating such behaviour if others have been rewarded for such behaviour (**vicarious reinforcement**).

The behavioural approach to psychopathology

Only behaviour is important – The **behavioural approach** focuses only on *behaviours*; the observable responses that a person makes to their environment. For example, someone with **obsessive-compulsive disorder (OCD)** might display compulsive behaviours such as constant hand washing, or someone with a **phobia** (phobic disorder) may display extreme **anxiety** in the presence of the phobic object.

Abnormal behaviours are learned – Abnormal behaviour is no different to normal behaviour in terms of how it is learned.

- For example, a psychological disorder might be produced when a **maladaptive behaviour** (such as a panic attack) leads to the desired increased attention for the individual (**operant conditioning**).
- Abnormal behaviours may also be acquired by seeing others rewarded for the same behaviour (**social learning theory**).

Learning environments – The environments in which behaviours are learned may reinforce maladaptive behaviours.

- For example, for an individual with **agoraphobia**, not leaving home lowers anxiety, and for those with **depression**, depressive behaviours may elicit help from others.
- Therefore, such behaviours may be learned because they are actually *adaptive* for the individual in those environments.

⬡ Limitations of the behavioural approach

A limited view – Behaviourist explanations have been criticised for offering an extremely limited view of the factors that might cause abnormal behaviours. Behaviourist explanations tend to ignore the role of physiological or cognitive factors in the onset and treatment of abnormality, both of which have been shown to have an important role to play in the emergence of psychopathology and in its treatment.

Counter evidence – One of the strengths of this approach is that it lends itself to scientific validation. However, research does not always support its claims. For example, explanations of the acquisition of phobic behaviours that focus on the role of conditioning in the development of these behaviours struggle to explain why so many people with a phobia cannot recall an incident in their past which led to traumatic conditioning or even any contact with the feared object.

The symptoms not the cause – Part of the success of this approach comes from the effectiveness of behavioural therapies for treating abnormal behaviour. However, such therapies treat only the symptoms, and the cause may still remain and simply resurface, albeit in a different form. This suggests that although the *symptoms* of many disorders are behavioural, the *cause* may not be.

↻ PUTTING IT ALL TOGETHER

Behaviourists believe that our actions are determined largely by the experiences we have in life, rather than by underlying pathology (the biological approach) or unconscious forces (the psychodynamic approach). Abnormality is seen as the development of behaviour patterns (through conditioning or through social learning) that are considered maladaptive for the individual.

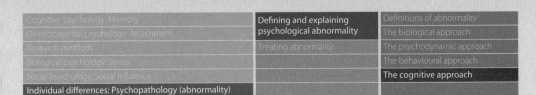

Cognitive psychology: Memory	Defining and explaining psychological abnormality	Definitions of abnormality
Developmental psychology: Attachment		The biological approach
Research methods	Treating abnormality	The psychodynamic approach
Biological psychology: Stress		The behavioural approach
Social psychology: Social influence		The cognitive approach
Individual differences: Psychopathology (abnormality)		

▲ *The cognitive model emphasises the importance of cognitive processing in psychological adjustment. The sleeping dog, whose real nature is unknown, is seen differently by two cats.*

KEY TERMS

A-B-C model
- Refers to the three components of experience that can be used to judge whether an individual's belief system is distorted.
- A for activating event – an event that we might encounter and can describe objectively.
- B for belief – what an individual believes is the truth about an event. This might include predictions about what any consequences might be.
- C for consequences – the feelings experienced as a result of beliefs associated with an event.

Cognitive approach to psychopathology
- Psychopathological behaviour is explained in terms of irrational and negative thinking about the world.
- If this faulty thinking can be changed, the problem will disappear.

Cognitive distortions
- Dysfunctional thought processes.
- For example processing information in a way likely to cause anxiety, or drawing faulty conclusions after processing information.

The cognitive approach to psychopathology

Abnormality is caused by faulty thinking – The **cognitive approach to psychopathology** assumes that thinking, expectations and attitudes (i.e. cognitions) direct behaviour.

- Mental illness is the result of **cognitive distortions** in the way a person thinks about a problem.
- Faulty and irrational thinking prevents the individual behaving adaptively.

The A-B-C model (**Ellis**, 1962)
- **A** refers to an **activating event** (e.g. the sight of a large dog).
- **B** is the **belief**, which may be rational (e.g. 'the dog is harmless') or irrational (e.g. 'the dog will attack me').
- **C** is the **consequence** – rational beliefs lead to healthy emotions (e.g. amusement) and irrational beliefs lead to unhealthy emotions (e.g. fear).

The individual is in control – Unlike the other three models, where abnormal behaviour is thought to be *determined* by factors outside the individual's control (e.g. **genetic** or environmental factors), the cognitive model portrays the individual as being the cause of their own behaviour, because they control their own thoughts. Abnormality is the result of faulty control of this process.

Limitations of the cognitive approach

Blames the patient – The cognitive model suggests it is the patient who is responsible, therefore overlooks situational factors, such as life stressors. By focusing only on events in the patient's mind, the implication is that recovery is only possible by changing the way the person thinks about these stressors, rather than changing the stressors themselves. Research on stress suggests that complete recovery must also target the sources of stress in a person's life.

Consequence rather than cause – It is not clear which comes first, i.e. do **maladaptive** thoughts cause mental disorder, or does mental disorder lead to faulty thinking? It is possible that an individual develops a negative way of thinking because of their disorder (as happens in depression). It is also possible that faulty thinking is a vulnerability factor for psychopathology, with individuals with maladaptive cognitions being at greater risk of developing mental disorders.

Irrational beliefs may be realistic – Not all irrational beliefs are 'irrational'. **Alloy and Abrahmson** suggest that many people with **depression** actually have a much more realistic view of the world than non-depressives. They found that depressed people gave much more accurate estimates of the likelihood of a disaster than 'normal' controls (the 'sadder but wiser' effect).

PUTTING IT ALL TOGETHER

The cognitive model of psychopathology emphasises that cognitive distortions may be at the root of many psychological disorders, particularly those that involve irrational and negative thinking. Distortions in the way we process information have been implicated in depression, **schizophrenia** and other mental disorders.

Cognitive psychology: Memory		Defining and explaining psychological abnormality	Biological therapies
Developmental psychology: Attachment			Psychological therapies – Psychoanalysis
Research methods		Treating abnormality	
Biological psychology: Stress			Psychological therapies – Systematic desensitisation
Social psychology: Social influence			
Individual differences: Psychopathology (abnormality)			Psychological therapies – CBT

KEY TERMS

Antipsychotics
- Drugs that are effective in the treatment of psychotic illnesses, such as schizophrenia.

Benzodiazepines (BZs)
- Drugs that have a tranquillising effect and are commonly used in the treatment of anxiety.

Beta-blockers (BBs)
- Drugs that block the action of adrenaline and noradrenaline during **sympathetic arousal**.

ECT
- Electro-convulsive shock therapy.
- Involves the administration of an electrical current through electrodes on the scalp.
- This induces a seizure, which can be effective in relieving an episode of major depression.

SSRIs
- Selective serotonin re-uptake inhibitors, a class of drug used in the treatment of **depression**.

⟳ PUTTING IT ALL TOGETHER

The biological approach proposes that the cause of psychopathology lies in underlying physiological processes, so it makes sense for the treatment to also be physical. Thus, biological therapies target physiological processes, such as the functioning of neurotransmitters, hormones and parts of the brain.

Biological therapies

⬡ Drugs

Antipsychotic drugs are used to combat the symptoms of psychotic illnesses such as **schizophrenia**. Conventional **antipsychotics** block the transmission of **dopamine**, and so alleviate many of the symptoms of this disorder.

Antidepressant drugs – SSRIs work by blocking the transporter mechanism that reabsorbs **serotonin** into the nerve cell, thus prolonging its activity and relieving the symptoms of depression.

Anti-anxiety drugs – Benzodiazepines reduce anxiety by slowing down activity of the central nervous system. **Beta-blockers** reduce the activity of **adrenaline** and **noradrenaline**, part of the body's response to stress.

⬡ Evaluation

Strengths
Effectiveness – Research suggests that chemotherapies do work when compared to **placebo** conditions. However, drugs alone are less effective than drugs combined with psychological therapies.

Ease of use – Drug therapies require little effort from the patient, therefore they are likely to be more motivated to continue treatment compared to more time-consuming psychological treatments.

Limitations
Tackle symptoms rather than cause – Drugs only offer temporary alleviation of symptoms. As soon as the patient stops taking the drug, its effectiveness ceases and the symptoms return.

Side effects – All drugs have side effects, e.g. SSRIs can cause nausea and suicidal thoughts. This is one of the main reasons drug treatments fail, as patients stop taking their medication because they can no longer stand the side effects.

⬡ ECT

ECT is generally used for severely **depressed** patients for whom psychotherapy and drug medication have proved ineffective.

How does it work? A small amount of electric current, lasting about half a second, is passed through the brain. This current produces a seizure, which affects the whole brain.

Why does it work? ECT causes changes in the way the brain works, but there is disagreement about the exact effects that lead to improvement. ECT affects the action of **neurotransmitters**, so recovery from depression may be a consequence of improving communication between different parts of the brain.

⬡ Evaluation

Strengths
ECT can save lives – ECT can be an effective treatment, particularly in cases of severe depression. As a result, it can be life-saving, especially when depression is so severe that it could lead to suicide.

Effectiveness – Comer states that 60–70% of ECT patients improve after treatment, although critics have also suggested that 84% of these patients had relapsed within six months of receiving ECT.

Limitations
Sham ECT – Studies that have compared the use of 'sham' ECT with real ECT have found that those receiving real ECT were more likely to recover. Some sham patients also recovered, suggesting that attention plays a part in recovery.

Side effects – Possible side effects include impaired memory, **cardiovascular** problems and headaches. A report from the **DOH** found that for those receiving ECT over the previous two years, 30% reported that it had left them with permanent fear and anxiety.

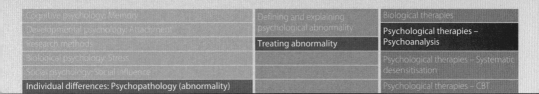

		Biological therapies
Cognitive psychology: Memory	Defining and explaining psychological abnormality	**Psychological therapies – Psychoanalysis**
Developmental psychology: Attachment	Treating abnormality	
Research methods		
Biological psychology: Stress		Psychological therapies – Systematic desensitisation
Social psychology: Social influence		
Individual differences: Psychopathology (abnormality)		Psychological therapies – CBT

KEY TERMS

False memories
- Remembering events, especially traumatic events, that have not actually occurred.
- May be prompted by the suggestion of a therapist.

Neurotic illness
- Describes a **nonpsychotic** mental illness that triggers feelings of distress and **anxiety** and impairs functioning.

Psychoanalysis
- A therapy developed by Sigmund Freud to make the unconscious conscious and deal with the causes of abnormal behaviour.
- Individuals are generally unaware of the many factors, some of which are unconscious, that cause their behaviour and affect their mental health.

Spontaneous remission
- The disappearance of psychopathological symptoms over time without formal treatment.

 Ethics

Psychoanalysis as a therapy is potentially fraught with **ethical** problems. These include the stress of *insight,* as painful memories are brought into the conscious mind, and the controversy of *false memories* (see below right).

⟳ PUTTING IT ALL TOGETHER

The psychological approach to treatment focuses more on psychological dimensions of behaviour (how people think and feel) than does the biological approach. Psychoanalysis attempts to help patients become aware of long-repressed unconscious feelings and issues that are contributing to their current **maladaptive** behaviour.

Psychological therapies – Psychoanalysis

Repression and the unconscious mind – Many of the factors that cause behaviour operate at an unconscious level, and are the result of **repressed** memories or unresolved conflicts from childhood. During **psychoanalysis**, the therapist attempts to trace these influences to their origins and help the individual to deal with them.

How does it work?

Free association – The patient expresses thoughts exactly as they occur, even though they may appear unimportant to the individual. This is intended to reveal areas of conflict and to bring memories that have been repressed into consciousness. The therapist then helps to interpret these memories, and the individual may add further thoughts and feelings.

Therapist interpretation – The therapist draws tentative conclusions about the possible cause(s) of the problem. Patients may offer resistance to these conclusions (e.g. by changing the subject), or may display transference, where they recreate feelings associated with the problem and transfer these feelings onto the therapist.

Working through – Patient and therapist examine the same issues over and over again in an attempt to gain greater clarity concerning the causes of their problematic behaviour. Freud believed this was the process that produced the greatest changes in the patient, and distinguished psychoanalytic treatment from any other type of psychological therapy.

⬡ Evaluation

Strengths

Effectiveness – An analysis of 10,000 patient histories estimated that 80% benefitted from psychoanalysis compared to 60% who received therapies based on different approaches (**Bergin**). This provides modest support for the effectiveness of psychoanalysis as a treatment for **neurotic illnesses**.

Length of treatment – A study of 450 patients by **Tschuschke *et al.*** found that psychodynamic therapies, such as psychoanalysis, were more effective in the long term. The longer the psychotherapeutic treatments took, the better the outcomes were, indicating that it takes motivation and effort from the patient for the treatment to be truly effective.

Limitations

No better than placebo – A therapy is only as good as the underlying theory. **Eysenck** argued that 'the obvious failure of Freudian therapy to significantly improve on **spontaneous remission** or **placebo** treatment is the clearest proof we have of the inadequacy of Freudian theory'. Eysenck also points out that the success of behavioural therapies casts further doubts on the **validity** of psychoanalysis as a useful treatment.

Appropriateness – When developing psychoanalysis as a therapy, Freud failed to appreciate the differences between individuals in the way that modern psychotherapists do. The development of humanistic therapies addressed this problem by putting the client first, adjusting the therapy to suit the individual client rather than imposing specific theories on them.

False memories – Critics of psychoanalysis claim that some therapists are not helping patients to recover *repressed* memories, but are unwittingly planting **false memories** of sexual abuse or even alien abduction. All psychoanalysis assumes that a patient can reliably recall early memories that have been repressed, but as yet there is little evidence to support this.

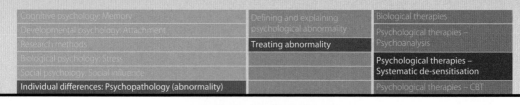

Cognitive psychology: Memory	Defining and explaining psychological abnormality	Biological therapies
Developmental psychology: Attachment		Psychological therapies – Psychoanalysis
Research methods	Treating abnormality	
Biological psychology: Stress		Psychological therapies – Systematic de-sensitisation
Social psychology: Social influence		
Individual differences: Psychopathology (abnormality)		Psychological therapies – CBT

KEY TERMS

Systematic desensitisation

- Based on **classical conditioning** (the **behavioural approach**).
- A therapy used to treat phobias and problems involving anxiety.
- A client is gradually exposed to the threatening situation under relaxed conditions until the anxiety reaction is extinguished.

Step 1: Patient is taught how to relax their muscles completely. (A relaxed state is incompatible with anxiety.)

Step 2: Therapist and patient together construct a desensitisation heierarchy – a series of imagined scenes, each one causing a little more anxiety than the previous one.

Step 3: Patient gradually works his/her way through desensitisation hierarchy, visualising each anxiety-evoking event while engaging in the competing relaxation response.

Step 4: Once the patient has mastered one step in the hierarchy (i.e. they can remain relaxed while imagining it), they are ready to move onto the next.

Step 5: Patient eventually masters the feared situation that caused them to seek help in the first place.

↻ PUTTING IT ALL TOGETHER

Systematic desensitisation is derived from the behavioural approach and is based on the principles of classical conditioning. SD is a counter-conditioning procedure whereby a fear response to an object or situation is gradually replaced with a relaxation response.

Psychological therapies – Systematic desensitisation (SD)

Systematic desensitisation is used in the treatment of anxiety, particularly anxiety associated with **phobias**. The aim of SD is to reduce, or even eliminate, the anxiety that people associate with feared objects or situations and which interferes with their ability to lead a normal, happy life. SD works by expanding the exposure time and gradually introducing the person to the feared situation, one bit at a time so it is not overwhelming.

How does it work?

- The patient is first taught how to relax, and then works through their desensitisation hierarchy with the aim of being able to relax and so reduce their anxiety at each stage.
- Achieved by introducing feared object/situation *gradually*, working through a hierarchy of scenes, each causing more anxiety than the previous one.
- Individuals can overcome their anxieties by learning to relax in the presence of stimuli that had previously made them anxious.
- The two responses of relaxation and fear are incompatible and the fear is eventually dispelled.
- SD can also work without presenting the feared stimulus but having the client *imagine* it.

⬡ Evaluation

Strengths

Appropriateness – Behavioural therapies, such as SD, are relatively quick and require less effort on the patient's part than other psychotherapies. Patients are more likely to persevere, making treatment more likely to succeed. SD can also be self-administered by using computer simulations. This has the potential to make delivery of this form of treatment even more efficient for the patient.

Effectiveness – SD is successful for a range of anxiety disorders, such as fear of flying. **Capafóns et al.** found that people with **aerophobia** had less anxiety after SD compared with a control group and also showed lower physiological signs of fear during a flight simulation. **McGrath et al.** estimate that SD is effective in about 75% of patients with phobias.

Limitations

Symptom substitution – SD may *appear* to resolve a problem, but simply eliminating symptoms (rather than dealing with the *cause* of **anxiety**) may result in other symptoms appearing later on. However, **Langevin** argues that, as yet, there is no evidence to support the claim that symptoms can be substituted in this way.

Not universally effective – SD appears to be less effective in treating anxieties that have an underlying adaptive component (e.g. fear of dangerous animals) than those that are acquired as a result of personal experience. The reason for this difference is most probably that these 'ancient' fears helped our ancestors to survive, therefore are harder to remove, even for modern humans.

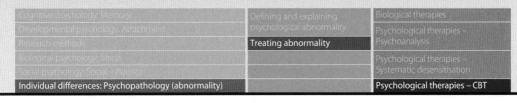

Cognitive psychology: Memory	Defining and explaining psychological abnormality	Biological therapies
Developmental psychology: Attachment		Psychological therapies – Psychoanalysis
Research methods	Treating abnormality	
Biological psychology: Stress		Psychological therapies – Systematic desensitisation
Social psychology: Social influence		
Individual differences: Psychopathology (abnormality)		Psychological therapies – CBT

Psychological therapies – Cognitive behavioural therapy

Cognitive behavioural therapies (CBT), such as **REBT**, are based on the idea that many problems are the result of irrational thinking. REBT helps the client understand this irrationality and the consequences of thinking in this way. It enables them to change any self-defeating thoughts and become happier and less anxious.

How does it work?

- Because irrational **b**eliefs (B) about **a**ctivating events (A) have unhealthy **c**onsequences (C), REBT tries to change these irrational beliefs into more rational beliefs. This leads to a more healthy emotional state and more positive behaviours.

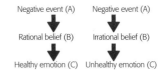

Negative event (A)   Negative event (A)
↓   ↓
Rational belief (B) Irrational belief (B)
↓   ↓
Healthy emotion (C) Unhealthy emotion (C)

- During therapy, the patient is encouraged to dispute self-defeating beliefs.
- Change is achieved through *logical* disputing (showing that the beliefs do not follow logically from the information available); *empirical* disputing (beliefs may not be consistent with reality) and *pragmatic* disputing (showing the lack of usefulness of existing beliefs).
- Person then moves to more rational interpretations of events. This adds an extension to the ABC model – **d**isputing (D), a more **e**ffective attitude to life (E) and a new set of **f**eelings (F).

Evaluation

Strengths

Appropriateness – A particular strength of REBT is that its usefulness is not limited to people suffering from mental disorders, but is also useful for non-clinical populations (e.g. people suffering from examination anxiety). REBT can be effective even in the absence of an actual therapist. For example, **Yoichi *et al.*** developed a computer-based counselling programme based on REBT that has produced significant decreases in anxiety.

Effectiveness – In a **meta-analysis** by **Engels *et al.***, REBT was shown to be effective in the treatment of a number of different types of disorder, including **OCD** and **agoraphobia**. REBT was more effective in the treatment of anxiety disorders than SD or a combination of other therapies.

Limitations

Irrational environments – REBT fails to address irrational environments that exist beyond the therapeutic situation (e.g. a bullying boss), which continue to produce and reinforce irrational thoughts and maladaptive behaviour.

Not suitable for all – REBT does not always work and is not always what people want. Some people fail to put the principles into practice and others do not want the 'direct' sort of advice of REBT.

Ethical issues in treatment – Disputing what appears to be an irrational belief 'to the therapist' may create difficulties for a client for whom this irrational belief is based on a fundamental religious belief.

PUTTING IT ALL TOGETHER

Rational-emotive behaviour therapy (REBT) is derived from the cognitive approach and focuses on changing the irrational thoughts that determine maladaptive behaviour. REBT emphasises that only part of the emotional disturbance people experience is caused by the activating event itself. The main cause of these disturbances are people's irrational beliefs and the fact that they continue to upset themselves with these thoughts. REBT aims to identify these irrational beliefs and by actively disputing them help to remove them and keep them removed.

Glossary

A-B-C model Refers to the three components of experience that can be used to judge whether an individual's belief system is distorted. A (activating event) leads to B (belief) and ultimately C (consequences). (page 63)

ACTH *see* Adrenocorticotrophic hormone.

Adrenal cortex A region of the adrenal gland, located above the kidneys. The adrenal cortex (outer region) manufactures glucocortoids (such as cortisol) and various sex hormones, such as testosterone. (page 42)

Adrenal medulla A region of the adrenal gland, located above the kidneys. The adrenal medulla (inner region) produces adrenaline and noradrenaline. (page 42)

Adrenaline A hormone associated with arousal of the autonomic nervous system (e.g. raised heart rate). It is also a neurotransmitter. Americans use the term 'epinephrine'. (pages 42, 50, 64)

Adrenocorticotrophic hormone (ACTH) A hormone produced in the pituitary gland as a response to stress. Its principal effect is the release of cortisol from the adrenal cortex. (page 42)

Aerophobia Fear of flying. (page 66)

Agentic shift People may move from being in a state where they take personal responsibility for their actions (an autonomous state) to a state where they believe they are acting on behalf of an authority figure (an agentic state). (page 55)

Agentic state A state where people believe they are acting on behalf of an authority figure. (page 55)

Agoraphobia Fear of being in places or situations from which escape might be difficult. (pages 62, 67)

Aim A statement of what the researcher(s) intend to find out in a research study. Often confused with hypothesis. (page 33)

Animal experiment An experiment using non-human animals, often conducted because of ethical issues involving the use of human participants. (pages 23, 24)

Anonymity An important aspect of confidentiality, a participant remains anonymous, i.e. their name is withheld or simply not recorded. (page 36)

ANS *see* Autonomic nervous system.

Anti-Semitism Hostility and prejudice towards Jews. (page 55)

Anticonformity The refusal or failure to conform to the generally accepted standards, conventions or rules of a group. (page 56)

Antigens Molecules (such as bacteria, viruses, toxins) which invade the body and are targeted by the immune system. (page 43)

Antipsychotics Drugs that are effective in the treatment of psychotic illnesses, such as schizophrenia. (page 64)

Anxiety A nervous emotional state where we fear that something unpleasant is about to happen. People often become anxious when they are in stressful situations. Anxiety tends to be accompanied by physiological arousal (e.g. a pounding heart and rapid shallow breathing). (pages 19, 27, 44, 50, 62, 65, 66)

Articulatory process A component of the phonological loop which acts as an 'inner voice', i.e. words/sounds are verbally repeated. (page 17)

Articulatory suppression task An activity which prevents rehearsal of words in the articulatory loop. (page 17)

Atherosclerosis The thickening of walls of the arteries which may lead to a heart attack. (page 43)

Attachment An emotional bond between two people that endures over time. Leads to certain behaviours such as clinging and proximity-seeking. Serves the function of protecting an infant. (pages 23, 26, 27, 28)

Attachment disorder A psychiatric disorder characterised by an individual's inability to identify a preferred attachment figure. (page 28)

Attribution When observing behaviour (our own or someone else's) we provide explanations for the behaviour. These explanations will be dispositional or situational. (page 37)

Attrition The loss of participants from a study over time. This is likely to leave a biased sample or a sample that is too small. (page 37)

Autonomic nervous system (ANS) governs the body's involuntary activities (e.g. stress, heart beat) and is self-regulating (autonomous). It is divided into the sympathetic branch (fight or flight) and the parasympathetic branch (rest and digest). (pages 42, 43)

Autonomous state A state where people take personal responsibility for their actions. (page 55)

Bar chart The height of each bar represents the frequency of that item. The categories are placed on the horizontal (*x* axis) and frequency is on the vertical (*y* axis). Bar charts are suitable for words and numbers (nominal or ordinal/interval data). (page 38)

BBs *see* Beta-blockers.

Behaviour checklist A systematic method for recording observations where a list of behavioural categories is used. The observer(s) can note every time any behaviour on the checklist is observed. (page 34)

Behavioural approach to psychopathology Behaviourists believe that normal *and* abnormal behaviours are acquired as a result of experiences that we have in life. Abnormal behaviours are learned through the processes of conditioning and social learning. (pages 62, 66)

Behavioural categories Dividing a target behaviour (such as attachment or sociability) into a subset of component behaviours to enable objective and reliable observations of the target behaviour. (pages 34, 35, 39)

Benzodiazepines (BZs) A group of drugs that have a tranquillising effect and are used to treat anxiety and stress. They work by slowing down the activity of the central nervous system. (pages 50, 64)

Beta-blockers (BBs) A drug that decreases anxiety by blocking the action of adrenaline and noradrenaline during sympathetic arousal. (pages 50, 64)

Biological approach to psychopathology Explains behaviour in terms of physiological and/or genetic causes. A mental disorder represents the consequences of a malfunction of biological processes. (page 60)

Brain scanning A variety of techniques used to investigate brain functioning by taking images of a living brain. This makes it possible to match regions of the brain to behaviour by asking participants to engage in particular activities while the scan is taking place. (page 16)

Buffer Something (e.g. a physical barrier or an ideological justification) that protects an individual from perceiving the true impact of their actions. (pages 54, 55)

BZs see Benzodiazepines.

Capacity A measure of how much can be held in memory. Measured in terms of bits of information such as number of digits. (pages 14, 16)

Cardiovascular disorder Disorders of the heart or circulatory system, including hypertension (high blood pressure, and heart disease). (pages 42, 43, 46, 50, 64)

Case study A research method that involves a detailed study of a single individual, institution or event. (pages 16, 17, 27, 28, 61)

CBT see Cognitive behavioural therapy.

Central executive Monitors and coordinates all other mental functions in the working memory model. (page 17)

Central nervous system (CNS) Comprises the brain and the spinal cord. (page 50)

CHD see Coronary heart disease.

Chunking Miller proposed that the capacity of STM can be enhanced by grouping sets of digits or letters into meaningful units or 'chunks'. (page 15)

CI see Cognitive interview.

Classical conditioning In classical conditioning, the neutral stimulus (NS) becomes the CS after the NS has been paired with the unconditioned stimulus. The NS now takes on the properties of a conditioned stimulus (CS) which produces a CR. (pages 23, 62, 66)

Clinical interview A form of unstructured or semi-structured interview, where the interviewer may start with a few prepared questions but further questions develop in response to the answers provided by the interviewee. Similar to the interview conducted when you consult your doctor. (page 34)

Closed question Question that has a range of answers from which respondents select one; produces quantitative data. (page 34)

Coding system A systematic method for recording observations in which individual behaviours are given a code for ease of recording. (page 34)

Cognitive approach to psychopathology Psychopathological behaviour is explained in terms of irrational and negative thinking about the world. If this faulty thinking can be changed, the problem will disappear. (page 63)

Cognitive behavioural therapy (CBT) A combination of cognitive therapy (to change maladaptive thoughts and beliefs) and behavioural therapy (to change behaviour in response to these thoughts and beliefs). (pages 49, 67)

Cognitive distortions Dysfunctional thought processes. For example, processing information in a way likely to cause anxiety, or drawing faulty conclusions after processing information. (page 63)

Cognitive interview (CI) A police technique for interviewing witnesses to a crime, based on what psychologists have found out about memory. (page 20)

Cohort effects One group of participants (cohort) may have unique characteristics because of time-specific experiences during their development, such as being a child during the Second World War. This may act as an extraneous variable. (page 40)

Collectivist culture Any culture which places more value on the 'collective' rather than on the individual, and on interdependence rather than on independence. The opposite is true of individualist culture. (pages 26, 52, 59)

Compliance Going along with others to gain their approval or avoid their disapproval. This is a result of social comparison, which enables an individual to adjust their behaviour to that of the group. There is no change in the person's underlying attitude; only their public behaviour. (pages 52, 53)

Conclusions The implications drawn from a study; what the findings tell us about people in general rather than just about the particular participants in a study. (pages 34, 39, 52)

Concordance rates A measure of similarity between two individuals or sets of individuals on a given trait, usually expressed as a percentage. (page 60)

Concurrent validity Establishing validity by comparing an existing method of measurement (e.g. test, questionnaire) with the one you are interested in. (page 35)

Conditioned response (CR) In classical conditioning, the response elicited by the conditioned stimulus, i.e. a new association has been learned so that the neutral stimulus (NS) produces the unconditioned response (UCR) which is now called the CR. (page 23)

Conditioned stimulus (CS) In classical conditioning, the neutral stimulus (NS) becomes the CS after the NS has been paired with the unconditioned stimulus. The NS now takes on the properties of the unconditioned stimulus (UCS) and produces the unconditioned response (now a conditioned response, CR). (page 23)

Confederate An individual in a study who is not a real participant and has been instructed how to behave by the investigator/experimenter. (pages 52, 54, 56)

Confidentiality A participant's right to have personal information protected. The Data Protection Act makes confidentiality a legal right. (page 36)

Conformity A form of social influence that results from exposure to the majority position and leads to compliance with that position. It is the tendency for people to adopt the behaviour, attitudes and values of other members of the group. (page 52)

Content analysis A kind of observational study in which behaviour is observed indirectly in written or verbal material such as interviews, conversations, books, diaries or TV programmes. (page 39)

Continuity hypothesis The view that there is a link between an infant's attachment relationship and later behaviour. (pages 24, 25)

Control The degree to which workers perceive that they have control over important aspects of their work, such as deadlines, procedures, etc. (page 46)

Control condition/group The condition (in a repeated measures design) or group (in an independent groups design) that provides a baseline measure of behaviour without the experimental treatment (IV), so that the effect of the experimental treatment may be assessed. (page 33)

Controlled observation A form of investigation in which behaviour is observed but under controlled conditions, as opposed to a naturalistic observation. (pages 23, 24, 25, 34)

Coronary heart disease (CHD) Failure of blood vessels to supply adequate blood to the heart. (page 47)

Correlation The relationship between two variables. (pages 29, 44)

Correlation coefficient A number between –1 and +1 that tells us how closely the co-variables in a correlational analysis are related. (page 38)

Correlational analysis Determines the extent of a relationship between two co-variables. (pages 38, 45)

Corticotrophin-releasing factor (CRF) is a neurotransmitter involved in the stress response. It is released by the hypothalamus and triggers production of ACTH in the pituitary gland. (page 42)

Cortisol A hormone released by the adrenal glands that is produced when an animal is stressed. (pages 42, 43)

Counterbalancing An experimental technique used to overcome order effects. Counterbalancing ensures that each condition is tested first or second in equal amounts. (page 33)

Co-variable A variable in a correlational analysis that is believed to vary systematically with another co-variable. (page 38)

Covert observation Observing people without their knowledge, e.g. using one-way mirrors. This is done because participants are likely to change their behaviour if they know they are being observed. (pages 34, 36)

CR *see* Conditioned response.

CRF *see* Corticotrophin-releasing factor.

Cross-cultural study One group of participants representing one section of society (e.g. young people or working class people) are compared with participants from another group (e.g. old people or middle-class people). (page 24)

Cross-sectional study One group of participants representing one section of society (e.g. young people or working class people) are compared with participants from another group (e.g. old people or middle class people). (page 40)

CS *see* Conditioned stimulus.

Cultural relativism The view that ideas of normal and abnormal behaviour differ from culture to culture. (page 59)

Culture The rules, customs, morals and ways of interacting that bind together members of a society or some other collection of people. (page 26)

Daily hassles Those frustrating, irritating everyday experiences that occur regularly in our work, home and personal life. (pages 44, 45)

Daily uplifts The minor positive experiences of everyday life that often counter the negative effects of daily hassles. (page 45)

Day care A form of temporary care (i.e. not all day and night) not provided by parents. Usually takes place outside the home and includes childminding and day nurseries. (pages 27, 29)

Debriefing A post-research interview designed to inform participants about the true nature of a study, and to restore them to the state they were in at the start of the study. It may also be used to gain feedback about the procedures used in the study. (page 36)

Decay An explanation for forgetting – the memory trace in our brain disintegrates over time. (pages 14, 16)

Deception This occurs when a participant is not told the true aims of a study (e.g. what participation will involve). Thus the participants cannot give truly informed consent. (pages 36, 54)

Demand characteristics A cue that makes participants aware of what the researcher expects to find or how participants are expected to behave. (page 33)

Dependent variable (DV) Depends in some way on the independent variable (IV). The DV is measured to assess the effects of the IV. (page 33)

Depression A mental disorder characterised by a lowering of mood, often accompanied by difficulty thinking, concentrating and sleeping, as well as feelings of anxiety. (pages 27, 44, 45, 59, 60, 61, 62, 63, 64)

Deprivation dwarfism Children who experience emotional deprivation are often physically smaller. Emotional disturbance (stress) may affect the production of hormones, such as growth hormones, and lead to a kind of physical 'dwarfism'. (page 28)

Deviation from ideal mental health Abnormality is seen as deviating from an ideal of positive mental health. This includes a positive attitude toward the self and an accurate perception of reality. (page 59)

Deviation from social norms Abnormal behaviour is a deviation from unwritten rules about how one 'ought' to behave. Violation of these rules is considered abnormal. (page 59)

Diary method A method of investigating behaviour where participants keep a regular record of their experiences, thoughts and behaviour. (page 45)

Diathesis-stress model In the case of certain disorders, individuals inherit a vulnerability for the disorder (diathesis) which develops only if such individuals are exposed to difficult environmental conditions (stress). The greater the underlying vulnerability, the less stress is needed to trigger the disorder. (pages 43, 60)

Differential experience hypothesis The ability to distinguish between groups of people improves as contact with those groups increases. (page 19)

Digit span technique A technique to assess the span of immediate (short-term) memory. Participants are given progressively more digits in a list to see how many can be recalled. (page 15)

Directional hypothesis States the direction of a difference (e.g. bigger or smaller) or correlation (positive or negative). (page 33)

Disinhibited attachment A type of insecure attachment where children do not discriminate about people they choose as attachment figures. Such children will treat near-strangers with inappropriate familiarity (overfriendliness) and may be attention-seeking. (pages 25, 28)

Displacement An explanation for forgetting, where existing information is displaced out of memory by new information. (pages 14, 16)

Dopamine A neurotransmitter involved in the sensation of pleasure, unusually high levels are associated with schizophrenia. (page 64)

Double blind technique Neither the participant or researcher are aware of the research aims or other important details of a study, and thus have no expectations that might alter a participant's behaviour. (page 33)

Duration A measure of how long a memory lasts before it is no longer available. (pages 14, 16)

DV *see* Dependent variable.

Ecological validity A form of external validity; the ability to generalise a research effect beyond the particular setting in which it is demonstrated, to other settings. (pages 14, 35)

ECT (electro-convulsive shock therapy) The administration of an electrical current through electrodes on the scalp. This induces a seizure, which can be effective in relieving major depression. (page 64)

Ego The conscious, rational part of the personality. It develops because a young child must deal with the constraints of reality and so is governed by the reality principle. (page 61)

Ego defences Unconscious methods, such as repression and projection, which help protect the individual from feelings of anxiety. (page 61)

Encoding The way information is changed so it can be stored in memory. Information enters the brain via the senses (e.g. eyes and ears) and is then stored (encoded) in various forms, such as visual codes (like a picture), acoustic forms (sounds), or a semantic form (the meaning of the experience). (pages 14, 16)

Episodic buffer In the working memory model, a store that receives input from many sources, temporarily stores this information, then integrates it in order to construct a mental episode of what is being experienced right now. (page 17)

Ethical committee (also called institutional review board IRB). A group of people within a research institution that must approve a study before it begins. (page 36)

Ethical guidelines Concrete, quasi-legal documents that help to guide conduct within psychology. (page 36)

Ethical issues arise in research where there are conflicting sets of values between researchers and participants concerning the goals, procedures or outcomes of a research study. (pages 34, 36, 65)

EV *see* Extraneous variable.

Event sampling An observational technique: counting the number of times a certain behaviour (event) occurs. (page 34)

EWT *see* Eyewitness testimony.

Experiment A research method to investigate causal relationships by observing the effect of an independent variable on the dependent variable (*see* Lab, Field and Natural experiment). (page 50)

Experimental condition/group In a repeated measures design, the condition containing the independent variable, or in an independent groups design, the group of participants who receive the experimental treatment (the IV). (pages 33, 61)

Experimental realism The extent to which participants become involved in an experiment and become less influenced by cues about how to behave. (page 35)

Experimenter bias *see* Investigator bias.

Experimenter effect *see* Investigator effect.

External reliability Concerns consistency *over time* such that it is possible to obtain the same results on subsequent occasions when a measure is used. (page 35)

External validity Concerns the degree to which a research finding can be generalised to, for example, other settings (ecological validity), or other groups of people (population validity), and over time (historical validity). (pages 35, 54)

Externals (external control) Individuals who tend to believe that their behaviour and experience is caused by events outside their own control. (page 56)

Extraneous variable (EV) Any variable, other than the IV, which may potentially affect the DV and thereby confound the findings. Order effects, participant variables and situational variables may act as EVs. (page 35)

Eyewitness testimony (EWT) The evidence provided in court by a person who witnessed a crime, with a view to identifying the perpetrator of the crime. The accuracy of eyewitness recall may be affected during initial encoding, subsequent storage and/or eventual retrieval. (page 18)

Failure to function adequately Mentally healthy people are judged as being able to operate within certain acceptable limits. If abnormal behaviour interferes with daily functioning, it may be considered abnormal. (page 59)

False memories Remembering events, especially traumatic events that have not actually occurred. May be prompted by the suggestion of a therapist. (page 65)

Field experiment A controlled experiment that is conducted outside a laboratory (i.e. not in a specially designed environment). The experimenter goes to the participant rather than vice versa. The IV is still manipulated by the experimenter, and therefore causal relationships can be demonstrated. (page 32)

Fight or flight A term meaning an animal is energised to either fight or run away in response to a sudden (acute) stressor. (page 42)

fMRI (functional magnetic resonance imagining) A method used to scan brain activity while a person is performing a task. It enables researchers to detect which regions of the brain are rich in oxygen and thus are active. (page 17)

GABA (Gamma-amino-butyric-acid) A neurotransmitter that regulates excitement in the nervous system, thus acting as a natural form of anxiety reducer. (page 50)

Genetic inheritance The reception of genetically coded traits as a result of transmission from parent to offspring. (pages 60, 63)

Hardiness training The aim of hardiness training is to acquire the characteristics of a 'hardy' personality; to increase self-confidence and a sense of self-control within an individual's life. (page 49)

Hardy personality A type of personality, which provides a defence against the negative effects of stress. A person with hardy personality is high in control, commitment and challenge. (pages 48, 49)

Hawthorne effect The tendency for participants to alter their behaviour merely as a result of knowing that they are being observed. (page 40)

Hippocampus A structure in the subcortical (i.e. 'under' the cortex) area of each hemisphere of the forebrain, associated with memory. Part of the limbic system, therefore involved in motivation, emotion and learning. (page 16)

Historical validity A form of external validity; the ability to generalise a research effect beyond the particular historical period in which it was demonstrated, to other historical periods. (page 35)

Holocaust The systematic, bureaucratic, state-sponsored persecution and murder of approximately six million Jews by the Nazi regime and its collaborators. 'Holocaust' is a word of Greek origin meaning 'sacrifice by fire'. (page 55)

Hormones Chemical substances that circulate in the blood and only affect target organs. They are produced in large quantities but disappear very quickly. Their effects are slow in comparison to the nervous system, but very powerful. (pages 28, 47)

Hypothalamus A structure in the subcortical (i.e. 'under' the cortex) area of each hemisphere of the forebrain. It functions to regulate bodily temperature, metabolic processes such as eating, and other autonomic activities, including emotional responses. (page 42)

Hypothesis A precise and testable statement about the assumed relationship between variables. (page 33)

Id The irrational, primitive part of the personality. It demands immediate satisfaction and is ruled by the pleasure principle. (page 61)

Immune system Designed to defend the body against antigens (bacteria, viruses, toxins, etc.) that would otherwise invade it. White blood cells (leucocytes) identify and eliminate foreign bodies (antigens). (pages 42, 43)

Imposed etic A technique or theory that is developed in one culture and then used to study people in a different culture. Such a technique or theory may be meaningless when used with people who have had different experiences or have different values. (page 26)

Independence/independent behaviour Behaving in a way that shows freedom from any control or influence of other group members. (page 52)

Independent groups design An experimental design where participants are allocated to two (or more) groups, each one receiving a different treatment. (page 33)

Independent variable (IV) An event that is directly manipulated by the experimenter in order to observe its effects on the dependent variable (DV). (page 33)

Individualist culture A culture that values independence rather than reliance on others, in contrast to many non-Western cultures that could be described as collectivist. (pages 26, 52, 59)

Informational social influence The result of wanting to be right, i.e. looking to others for the right answer, and conforming to their opinion. (page 53)

Informed consent In terms of ethics, participants must be given comprehensive information concerning the nature and purpose of a study and their role in it. This is necessary in order that they can make an informed decision about whether to participate. (pages 36, 54)

Inner scribe In the working memory model, a component of the visuo-spatial sketchpad which deals with spatial relations, such as the arrangement of objects in the visual field. (page 17)

Insecure attachment Develops as a result of caregiver's lack of sensitive responding to the infant's needs. May be associated with poor cognitive and emotional development. (pages 25, 26, 29)

Insecure-avoidant attachment Infants who are willing to explore and are unresponsive to mother's return; they generally avoid social interaction and intimacy with others. (pages 25, 26)

Insecure-disorganised attachment Infants who lack consistent patterns of attachment behaviour. (page 25)

Insecure-resistant (ambivalent) attachment Infants are less interested in exploring and show distress on mother's return; generally they both seek and reject intimacy and social interaction. (pages 25, 26)

Institutional care An 'institution' is a place dedicated to a particular task, such as looking after children awaiting adoption, caring for the mentally ill or looking after patients in hospital. It is a place where people are looked after for a period of time, as opposed to day care or outpatient care where people go home every day. In the past, such institutions had fairly strict regimes and offered little emotional care. (page 28)

Inter-interviewer reliability The extent to which there is agreement between two or more interviewers in the answers they elicit from interviewees. (page 35)

Inter-observer reliability The extent to which there is agreement between two or more raters involved in rating a behaviour. (pages 35, 39)

Internal reliability Concerns consistency *within* a set of scores or items. (page 35)

Internal validity Concerns whether a study or measurement has tested what it set out to test. (pages 14, 35, 54)

Internal working model A cluster of concepts about relationships. In the short term, it gives a child insight into their caregiver's behaviour. In the long term, it acts as a template for future relationships because it generates expectations about how people behave. (page 24)

Internalisation Going along with others because of an acceptance of their point of view. This is a result of an examination of the group's position, which may lead to *validation* of the person's own views, or acceptance of the group's views both in public and in private. (pages 52, 53)

Internals (internal control) Individuals who tend to believe that they are responsible for their behaviour and experience (as distinct from external influences) (page 56)

Interval data Measured using units of equal intervals, such as when counting correct answers or using any 'public' unit of measurement. (page 38)

Intervening variable A variable that comes between two other variables that can explain the relationship between those two variables. (page 40)

Interview A research method or technique that involves a face-to-face, 'real-time' interaction with another individual and results in the collection of data. (page 34)

Interviewer bias The effect of an interviewer's expectations on a respondent's behaviour. Such expectations are communicated unconsciously. (page 35)

Investigator/experimenter bias The effect that an investigator/experimenter's expectations have on the participants and thus on the results of a research study. (page 40)

Investigator effect Where the investigator directly or indirectly has an effect on a participant's performance, other than what was intended. (page 33)

IV *see* Independent variable.

Lab experiment An experiment carried out in a controlled setting. Lab experiments tend to have high experimental (internal) validity and low ecological (external) validity, although this isn't always true. (pages 14, 15, 16, 17, 18, 19, 20, 21, 52, 54)

Leading question A question that, either by its form or content, suggests what answer is desired or leads to the desired answer. (page 34)

Learning theory The name given to a group of explanations, i.e. classical and operant conditioning. Essentially, these explain behaviour in terms of learning rather than any inborn tendencies (the biological/ evolutionary approach) or higher order thinking (the cognitive approach). (page 25)

Leucocytes White blood cells, the cells of the immune system that defend the body against infectious disease and foreign bodies. (page 43)

Levels of measurement The different ways of measuring something; the lower levels are less precise. (page 38)

Life change units (LCUs) A measure of the stress levels of different types of change experienced during a given period e.g. death of a spouse is scored at 100, divorce at 73. (page 44)

Life changes Events (e.g. divorce or bereavement) that require a significant adjustment in a person's life, thus they are a significant source of stress. (pages 44, 45)

Locus of control An aspect of our personality: people differ in their beliefs about whether the outcomes of their actions are contingent on what they do (internal control) or on events outside their personal control (external control). (page 56)

Long-term memory (LTM) Memory for events that have happened in the past. Lasts anywhere from 2 minutes to 100 years and has potentially unlimited duration and capacity. (pages 14, 16)

Longitudinal study Observation of the same items over a long period of time. (pages 24, 28, 29, 46)

LTM *see* Long-term memory.

Majority influence A form of social influence where people follow the norm established by the majority. (page 52)

Maladaptive behaviour Behaviours that inhibit a person's ability to cope with, or adjust to, particular situations. (pages 45, 59, 62, 63, 65)

Matched pairs design An experimental design where pairs of participants are matched in terms of key variables such as age and IQ. One member of each pair is placed in the experimental group and the other member in the control group. (page 33)

Maternal reflexive thinking Being able to understand what someone else is thinking.

Mean Calculated by adding up all the numbers and dividing by the number of numbers. It can only be used with interval or ratio data. (page 38)

Measures of central tendency A descriptive statistic that provides information about a 'typical' number for a data set. (page 38)

Measures of dispersion A descriptive statistic that provides information about how spread out a set of scores are. (page 38)

Median The middle value in an ordered list, suitable for ordinal or interval data. (page 38)

Meta-analysis A researcher looks at the findings from a number of different studies in order to reach a general conclusion about a particular hypothesis. (pages 19, 20, 26, 43, 47, 50, 52, 57, 67)

Minority influence A form of social influence where people reject the established norm of the majority of group members and move to the position of the minority. (page 57)

Misleading information Information that might suggest a particular answer to an eyewitness, thus leading them to provide inaccurate information. (page 18)

Mnemonic techniques Methods used to improve your memory for things. (page 21)

Mode The value that is most common. (page 38)

Monocausal emphasis Relying on just one causal factor when explaining an event. (page 55)

Monotropy The idea that the one relationship that the infant has with his/her primary attachment figure is of special significance in emotional development. (page 24)

Multi-store model (MSM) An explanation of memory based on three separate memory stores, and how information is transferred between these stores. (page 16)

Mundane realism Refers to how a study mirrors the real world. The experimental environment is realistic to the degree to which experiences encountered in the experimental environment will occur in everyday life (the 'real world'). (page 35)

Natural experiment A research method in which the experimenter cannot manipulate the independent variable directly, but where it varies as a consequence of some other action, and the effect on a dependent variable can be observed. (pages 14, 19, 28, 43, 44, 47)

Naturalistic observation A research method carried out in a naturalistic setting, in which the investigator does not interfere in any way, but merely observes the behaviour(s) in question (likely to involve the use of structured observations). (pages 25, 27, 34, 35)

Negative correlation As one co-variable increases, the other decreases. (page 38)

Neuroanatomy The branch of anatomy that deals with the structure of the brain and other parts of the nervous system. (page 60)

Neurochemistry The action of chemicals (e.g. neurotransmitters) in the brain and the drugs that influence neural activity. (page 60)

Neuron A specialised cell in the nervous system for transmission of information. (page 50)

Neurotic illness Describes a nonpsychotic mental illness that triggers feelings of distress and anxiety and impairs functioning. (page 65)

Neurotransmitter Chemical substances, such as serotonin or dopamine, which play an important part in the workings of the nervous system by transmitting nerve impulses across a synapse. (pages 50, 60, 64)

Neutral stimulus (NS) In classical conditioning, the stimulus that initially does not produce the target response, i.e. it is neutral. Through association with the unconditioned stimulus (UCS), the NS acquires the properties of the UCS and becomes a conditioned stimulus (CS) producing a conditioned response (CR). (page 23)

Nominal data Data in separate categories, such as grouping people according to their favourite football team. (page 38)

Non-directional hypothesis Predicting that there will be a difference between two conditions or two groups of participants, without stating the direction of the difference. (page 33)

Non-participant observation An observational study where the observer is not taking part in the activity being observed. (page 34)

Nonpsychotic illness A psychotic illness is one where a patient loses touch with reality, such as schizophrenia. Neurotic illnesses are nonpsychotic. (page 65)

Nonsense trigram A group of three letters that have no meaning. (page 14)

Noradrenaline A hormone associated with arousal of the autonomic nervous system (e.g. raised heart rate), and also a neurotransmitter. (pages 42, 50, 64)

Normative social influence The result of wanting to be liked and be accepted as part of a group by following its norms. (page 53)

NS *see* Neutral stimulus.

Obedience alibi Reaching a conclusion that obedience had a key role in Holocaust events when such a conclusion is unjustified given an analysis of the historical record. (page 55)

Obedience to authority A type of social influence whereby somebody acts in response to a direct order from a figure with perceived authority. There is also the implication that the person receiving the order is made to respond in a way that they would not have done without the order. (page 54)

Observation/observational techniques The application of systematic methods of observation in an observational study, experiment (to measure the DV) or other study. (page 39)

Observational learning Learning through observing others and imitating their behavior. (page 62)

Observer bias The tendency for observations to be influenced by expectations or prejudices. (page 35)

Obsessive-compulsive disorder (OCD) A mental disorder where anxiety arises from both obsessions (persistent and intrusive thoughts) and compulsions (means of controlling these thoughts). (pages 62, 67)

OCD *see* Obsessive-compulsive disorder.

Oedipal conflict Incestuous feelings that a young boy develops for his mother, coupled with rivalry with his father for her affections, leading to castration anxiety. Resolution of this conflict leads to the development of the superego. (page 61)

Open question A question that invites respondents to provide their own answers rather than to select an answer that has been provided. Tends to produce qualitative data. (page 34)

Operant conditioning Involves reinforcement each time you do something and it results in a pleasant consequence, the behaviour is 'stamped in' (reinforcement). It becomes more probable that you will repeat that behaviour in the future. If you do something and it results in an unpleasant consequence (punishment), it becomes less likely that you will repeat that behaviour. (page 62)

Operationalise Providing variables in a form that can be easily measured, i.e. the constituent operations are identified. (pages 33, 34)

Opportunity sample A sample of participants produced by selecting people who are most easily available at the time of the study. (page 37)

Order effects In a repeated measures design, an extraneous variable arising from the order in which conditions are presented. For example, participants do better the second time because they have had some practice. (page 33)

Ordinal data Data that is ordered in some way, for example asking people to put a list of football teams in order of liking. The 'difference' between each item is not the same, i.e. the individual may like the first item a lot more than the second, but there might only be a small difference between the items ranked second and third. (page 38)

Overt observation An observational technique where observations are 'open', i.e. the participants are aware that they are being observed. (page 34)

Own-age bias The tendency to recognise or remember things more easily if they relate to your own age group. (page 19)

Participant effects A general term used to acknowledge the fact that participants react to cues in an experimental situation and that this may affect the validity of any conclusions drawn from the investigation. (page 32)

Participant observation A kind of observational study where the observer is also a participant in the activity being observed. This may affect the objectivity of their observations. (page 34)

Participant variables Characteristics of individual participants (such as age, intelligence, etc.) that might influence the outcome of a study. (page 33)

Personal Views Survey A measure of 'hardiness'. The overall hardiness score is a composite of three subscales: commitment, control and challenge. (page 48)

Phobia A mental disorder characterised by high levels of anxiety that, when experienced, interfere with normal living. Includes specific and social phobias. (pages 62, 66)

Phonological loop A component of the working memory model that encodes speech sounds, involving maintenance rehearsal (repeating the words over and over, i.e. a *loop*). It is divided into a phonological store (inner ear) and an articulatory process (inner voice). (page 17)

Phonological store A component of the phonological loop which acts as an 'inner ear', i.e. storing sounds. (page 17)

Pilot study A small-scale trial of a study. Run to test any aspects of the design, with a view to making improvements. (page 34)

Pituitary-adrenal system Stress response involving the pituitary gland and adrenal medulla. It helps the body cope with chronic stressors. (pages 42, 43)

Pituitary gland Known as the 'master gland', the pituitary releases a variety of hormones that act on other glands throughout the body. (page 42)

Placebo A drug or treatment that contains no active ingredient or therapeutic procedure. (pages 50, 60, 64, 65)

Pleasure principle In Freudian psychology, the id's primitive desire to seek instant gratification and avoid pain at all costs. (page 61)

Population validity A form of external validity; the ability to generalise a research effect beyond the particular population from which the sample was drawn, to other populations. (page 35)

Positive correlation Co-variables increase together. (pages 29, 38)

Post-event information In eyewitness testimony, information supplied after the event, such as a leading question. (page 18)

Practice effect In a repeated measures design, participants may do better on one condition rather than another because they have completed it first and therefore may have improved their ability to perform the task. (page 33)

Predictive validity A means of establishing validity by considering the extent to which the current measure predicts (or correlates with) other measures of the same construct measured at some time in the future. (page 25)

Prefrontal cortex The anterior part of the frontal lobe, involved in 'executive functions', such as complex cognitive behaviours, moderating socially appropriate behaviours, personality and goal-directed behaviour (motivation). (page 16)

Presumptive consent A method of dealing with lack of informed consent or deception by asking a group of people who are similar to the participants whether they would agree to take part in a study. If this group of people consent to the procedures in the proposed study, it is *presumed* that the real participants would agree as well. (page 36)

Primacy effect The tendency to remember words from the start of a list. (page 16)

Primary attachment figure The person who has formed the closest bond with a child. Demonstrated by the intensity of the relationship. Usually a child's biological mother, but could be an adoptive mother, a father, grandmother, etc. (pages 24, 27)

Primary reinforcer An innate reinforcer. (page 23)

Privacy A person's right to control the flow of information about themselves. If privacy is invaded, confidentiality should be protected. (page 36)

Privation The failure to develop any attachments during early life. This is contrasted with 'deprivation' or 'disruption' where attachment bonds have formed, but may be disrupted either through physical or simply emotional separation. Such disruption may last for weeks or a lifetime (in the case of parental death). (pages 25, 28)

Projection A form of ego defence whereby a person unknowingly displaces unacceptable feelings on to someone or something else as a means of coping. (page 61)

Protection from harm During a research study, participants should not experience negative physical effects, such as physical injury. Nor psychological effects, such as lowered self-esteem or embarrassment. (pages 36, 54)

Psychoanalysis A therapy developed by Sigmund Freud to make the unconscious conscious and deal with the causes of abnormal behaviour. (page 65)

Psychodynamic approach to psychopathology Any approach that emphasises the dynamics of behaviour. In other words, what *drives* us to behave in particular ways. (page 61)

Punishment In operant conditioning, the application of an unpleasant stimulus such that the likelihood of the behaviour that led to it reoccurring is decreased. (page 23)

Qualitative data Expresses 'quality'. This includes descriptions, meanings, pictures and so on. The data cannot be counted or quantified but they can be turned into quantitative data by placing information in categories and counting instances. (pages 34, 39)

Qualitative data analysis Summarising qualitative data, for example by identifying themes and interpreting the meaning of an experience to the individual(s) concerned. (page 39)

Quantitative data Represents how much or how long, or how many, etc. there are of something. Data that are measured in numbers or quantities. (pages 34, 38, 39)

Quantitative data analysis Any means of representing trends from numerical data, such as measures of central tendency. (page 38)

Quasi-experiments Studies that are 'almost' experiments but lack one or more features of a true experiment, such as full experimenter control over the IV and random allocation of participants to conditions. This means that such studies cannot claim to demonstrate causal relationships. (page 19)

Questionnaire Data is collected through the use of written questions. (pages 19, 34, 43, 44, 46)

Quota sample Groups of participants are selected according to their frequency in the population. Selection is done from each group using opportunity sampling. (page 37)

Random allocation Allocating participants to experimental groups using random techniques. (page 33)

Random sample A sample of participants produced by using a random technique. (page 37)

Random technique Method of selection that ensures each member of the population has an equal chance of being selected. For example, placing all names in a hat and drawing out the required number, or by assigning each person a number and using a random number table. (page 37)

Range The difference between the highest and lowest score in a data set. (page 38)

Ratio data A level of measurement where there is a true zero point, as in most measures of physical quantities. (page 38)

Reality principle In psychoanalytic theory, the drive by the ego to accommodate the demands of the environment in a realistic way. (page 61)

REBT (Rational emotive behaviour therapy) A cognitive behavioural therapy that helps people change dysfunctional emotions and behaviours. It does this by making them aware of their self-defeating beliefs and replacing them with more constructive ones. (page 67)

Recency effect The tendency to remember words from the end of a list. (page 16)

Regression A form of ego defence whereby a person returns psychologically to an earlier stage of development rather than handling unacceptable impulses in a more adult way. Anxiety-provoking thoughts can thus be temporarily pushed into the unconscious. Often confused with repression. (page 61)

Reinforcement If a behaviour results in a pleasant state of affairs, the behaviour is 'stamped in' or reinforced. It is then more probable that the behaviour will be repeated in the future. Can be positive or negative reinforcement – both lead to an increased likelihood that the behaviour will be repeated. (page 23)

Reinforcer Anything that is experienced as rewarding. (page 23)

Reliability A measure of consistency. (pages 35, 44)

Repeated measures design An experimental design where each participant takes part in every condition under test. (page 33)

Repression A form of ego defence whereby anxiety-provoking material is kept out of conscious awareness as a means of coping. (pages 61, 65)

Right to withdraw Participants should have the right to withdraw from participating in a study if they are uncomfortable in any way. They should also have the right to refuse permission for the researcher to use any data they produced. (page 36)

Role play A controlled observation in which participants are asked to imagine how they would behave in certain situations, and then asked to act out the part. This method has the advantage of permitting the study of behaviours that might be unethical or difficult to find in the real world. (page 40)

Sampling The process of taking a sample. All sampling techniques aim to produce a representative selection of the target population. (pages 34, 35, 37, 39)

Scattergram A graphical representation of the relationship (i.e. the correlation) between two sets of scores. (page 38)

Schizophrenia A mental disorder where an individual has lost touch with reality and may experience symptoms such as delusions, hallucinations, grossly disorganised behaviour and flattened emotions. (pages 60, 64)

Scientific method The method used in scientific research where scientists start by observing natural phenomena and then develop explanations and hypotheses that are tested using systematic research methods. (page 40)

Secondary attachment figure Acts as a kind of emotional safety net, and is therefore important in emotional development. Also contributes to social development. (page 24)

Secondary reinforcer A reinforcer that is acquired through experience. (page 23)

Secure attachment An infant who is willing to explore, easy to soothe and displays high stranger anxiety. The infant is comfortable with social interaction and intimacy. Such attachments are related to healthy subsequent cognitive and emotional development. Develops as a result of sensitive responding by the primary attachment figure to the infant's needs. (pages 25, 26, 27)

Self-actualisation A person's motivation to maximise their achievements and fulfil their potential. (page 59)

Self-report technique A research method that relies on the participant answering questions – either verbally (in an interview) or in writing (in a questionnaire). (page 35)

Sensitive period A biologically-determined period of time during which a child is particularly sensitive to a specific form of stimulation, resulting in the development of a specific response or characteristic. (page 24)

Sensory memory (SM) Information at the senses – information collected by your eyes, ears, nose, fingers and so on. Information is retained for a very brief period by the sensory registers (less than half a second). Capacity of sensory memory is very large. The method of encoding depends on the sense organ involved, i.e. visual for the eyes, acoustic for the ears. (page 16)

Separation anxiety Distress shown by an infant when separated from his/her attachment figure. (page 25)

Serial position effect Information is recalled better from the most recently presented material (the recency effect) and from the first information presented (the primacy effect). (page 16)

Serotonin A neurotransmitter found in the central nervous system. Low levels have been linked to many different behaviours and physiological processes, including aggression, eating disorders and depression. (pages 60, 64)

Short-term memory (STM) Memory for immediate events. Lasts for a very short time and disappears unless rehearsed. Limited duration and limited capacity. Sometimes referred to as working memory. (pages 14, 15, 16)

Single blind technique A type of research design in which the participant is not aware of the research aims or of which condition of the experiment they are receiving. (page 33)

Situational variables Any factor in the environment that could affect the dependent variable, such as noise, time of day or the behaviour of an investigator. (page 33)

SM *see* Sensory memory.

SNS *see* Sympathetic nervous system.

Social change Occurs when a society as a whole adopts a new belief or way of behaving, which then becomes widely accepted as the norm. (page 57)

Social desirability bias The tendency for respondents to answer questions in a way that presents them in a better light. (page 35)

Social learning theory The assumption that people learn through indirect as well as direct rewards, by observing the behaviour of models (observational learning) and imitating such behaviour if others have been rewarded for such behaviour (vicarious reinforcement). (page 62)

Social releasers A social behaviour or characteristic that elicits a caregiving reaction. (page 24)

Split-half method A method of assessing internal reliability by comparing two halves of, for example, a psychological test to see if both halves produce a similar same score. (page 35)

Spontaneous remission The disappearance of psychopathological symptoms over time without formal treatment. (page 65)

SRRS (Social Readjustment Rating Scale) Developed by Holmes and Rahe to be able to test the idea that life changes are related to stress-related illnesses, such as anxiety and depression. (pages 44, 48)

SSRIs Selective serotonin re-uptake inhibitors, a class of drug used in the treatment of depression. (page 64)

Standard deviation Shows the amount of variation in a data set. It assesses the spread of the data around the mean. (page 38)

Standard interview An interview that lacks the four CI components. (page 20)

Standardised instructions The instructions given to participants to tell them how to perform a task. (page 40)

Standardised procedures A set of procedures that are the same for all participants in order to be able to repeat a study. This includes standardised instructions. (page 40)

STM *see* Short-term memory.

Strange Situation Method to assess strength of attachment, conducted in a novel environment and involving eight episodes. An infant's behaviour is observed as mother leaves and returns, and when with a stranger. Measures attachment in terms of stranger anxiety and separation anxiety. (page 25)

Stranger anxiety Distress shown by an infant when approached by an unfamiliar person. (page 25)

Stratified sample Groups of participants are selected according to their frequency in the population. Selection is done randomly from each strata. (page 37)

Stress Experienced when the perceived demands of a situation are greater than the perceived ability to cope. (pages 42, 44, 48, 49, 50, 60)

Stress inoculation training (SIT) A type of CBT which trains people to cope with stressful situations more effectively by learning skills to protect them from the damaging effects of future stressors. (page 49)

Stress management Techniques intended to help people deal more effectively with the stress in their lives so that they are less adversely affected by it. (page 49)

Structured interview Any interview in which the questions are decided in advance. (pages 34, 47)

Structured observation An observer uses various 'systems' to organise observations, such as behavioural categories and sampling procedures. (page 34)

Studies using a correlational analysis *see* Correlational analysis.

Suffragettes Women seeking the right to vote by means of organised protest. (page 57)

Superego This develops between the ages of three and six. It embodies the conscience and our sense of right and wrong, as well as notions of the ideal self. (page 61)

Sympathetic arousal/branch/nervous system (SNS) The part of the autonomic nervous system that is associated with physiological arousal and 'fight or flight' responses. (pages 42, 43, 64)

Sympathomedullary pathway A stress response, involving the SNS and adrenal cortex, which helps the body prepare for fight or flight. (pages 42, 43, 50)

Synaptic gap/synapse A small gap separating neurons. It consists of the presynaptic membrane (which discharges neurotransmitters), the postsynaptic membrane (containing receptor sites for neurotransmitters) and a synaptic gap between the two. The synaptic gap between a transmitting and receiving neuron is about 10 nm wide. (page 50)

Systematic desensitisation Based on classical conditioning (the behavioural approach), a therapy used to treat phobias and problems involving anxiety. A client is gradually exposed to the threatening situation under relaxed conditions until the anxiety reaction is extinguished. (pages 49, 66)

Systematic sample A method of obtaining a representative sample by selecting every, for example, 5th or 10th person. (page 37)

Target population The group of people that the researcher is interested in. The group of people from whom a sample is drawn and about whom generalisations can be made. (page 37)

Temperament hypothesis The view that attachment type can be explained in terms of an infant's innate temperament rather than caregiver sensitivity. (page 24)

Tend and befriend A response to stress that is more associated with females. It involves protecting the young (the 'tend' response) and seeking social contact and support from other females (the 'befriend' response). (page 42)

Terrorism Any act intended to cause death or serious bodily harm to civilians with the purpose of intimidating a population or compelling a government to do, or abstain from, any act. (page 57)

Test–retest reliability A method used to check external reliability. The same test or interview is given to the same participants on two occasions to see if the same results are obtained. (pages 35, 44)

Time sampling An observational technique in which the observer records behaviours in a given time frame, e.g. noting what a target individual is doing every 30 seconds, or some other time interval. (page 34)

Type A personality A tendency to approach life in a certain way, characterised by, for example, competitiveness and impatience. It is believed to increase the risk of coronary heart disease. (page 47)

Type B personality Characterised by an easygoing, relaxed and patient approach to life, it is believed to decrease the risk of coronary heart disease. (page 47)

UCR *see* Unconditioned response.

UCS *see* Unconditioned stimulus.

Unconditioned response (UCR) In classical conditioning, the innate reflex response to a stimulus, such as salivating when presented with food. (page 23)

Unconditioned stimulus (UCS) In classical conditioning, the stimulus that inevitably produces an innate reflex response, such as food producing a salivation response. (page 23)

Unstructured interview An interview that starts out with some general aims and possibly some questions, and lets the interviewee's answers guide subsequent questions. (page 34)

Unstructured observation An observer records all relevant behaviour but has no system. This technique may be chosen because the behaviour to be studied is largely unpredictable. (page 34)

Validity The extent to which a study and its findings are legitimate or true. (pages 18, 27, 34, 35, 44, 46, 65)

Vicarious reinforcement Learning which is not through direct reinforcement of behaviour, but through observing someone else being reinforced for that behaviour. (page 62)

Visual cache In the working memory model, a component of the visuo-spatial sketchpad which deals with the storage of visual information, such as the arrangement of objects. (page 17)

Visuo-spatial sketchpad In the working memory model, a component which encodes visual information. Divided into the visual cache (stores information) and inner scribe (spatial relations). (page 17)

Volunteer bias A form of sampling bias. Occurs because volunteer participants are usually more highly motivated than randomly selected participants. (page 37)

Volunteer sample A sample of participants produced by asking for volunteers. Sometimes referred to as a 'self-selected' sample. (page 37)

Weapon focus effect In violent crimes, an eyewitness' attention may be drawn to the weapon held by a criminal, reducing their ability to remember other details, such as the criminal's face. (page 19)

Withdrawal symptoms Abnormal physical or psychological reactions to the abrupt discontinuation of a drug to which an individual has developed physical dependence. (page 50)

Word-length effect People remember lists of short words better than lists of long words, governed by the capacity of the phonological loop. (page 17)

Working memory model (WMM) An explanation of short-term memory, called 'working memory'. Based on four components, some with storage capacity. (page 17)

Workload The demands of a person's work role. This can be stressful because it is repetitive, high intensity, monotonous or high volume. (page 46)

Workplace stressors Aspects of our working environment that we experience as stressful, and which cause a stress reaction in our body. (page 46)

Yerkes-Dodson law The curvilinear relationship between arousal and performance – people do not perform well when they are very relaxed, they perform best when moderately aroused and performance drops again at high levels of arousal. (page 19)

Zero correlation Co-variables are not linked. (page 38)

The Complete Companions for A Level Psychology

Written by an expert team of experienced authors and editors led by **Mike Cardwell** and **Cara Flanagan**

For AQA A

The Student Books

Psychology AS
The Complete Companion
Student Book
Mike Cardwell · Cara Flanagan

Psychology A2
The Complete Companion
Student Book
Mike Cardwell · Cara Flanagan

978 019 912981 2

978 019 912984 3

The Exam Companions

Psychology AS
The Exam Companion
Mike Cardwell · Cara Flanagan

Psychology A2
The Exam Companion
Mike Cardwell · Cara Flanagan

978 019 912982 9

978 019 912985 0

The Mini Companions

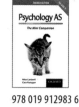
Psychology AS
The Mini Companion
Mike Cardwell
Cara Flanagan

Psychology A2
The Mini Companion
Mike Cardwell
Cara Flanagan

978 019 912983 6

978 019 912986 7

The AS Visual Companion

Psychology AS
The Visual Companion
Mike Cardwell
Cara Flanagan

978 185 008548 5

The Teacher's Companions

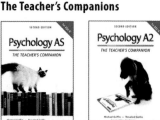

Psychology AS
THE TEACHER'S COMPANION
Michael Griffin · Rosalind Geills

Psychology A2
THE TEACHER'S COMPANION
Michael Griffin · Rosalind Geills

978 185 008295 8

978 185 008396 2

The AS Digital Companion

Psychology AS
The Digital Companion
Cara Flanagan · Pam Berkley · Jean-Marc Lawton

978 185 008394 8

The AS Audio Companion
CD-ROM with printable activity sheets and site licence

Psychology AS
The Audio Companion
Mike Cardwell · Cara Flanagan · Michael Griffin

978 019 912972 0

For WJEC

The Student Books

Psychology AS
The Complete Companion
Cara Flanagan · Lucy Marshall · Rhiannon Murray

Psychology A2
The Complete Companion
Cara Flanagan · Julia Russell

978 185 008440 2

978 185 0085713

The AS Revision Companion

Psychology AS
The Revision Companion
Cara Flanagan · Lucy Marshall · Rhiannon Murray

978 019 913617 9

For all A Level courses

Research Methods Companion

Research Methods Companion
for A Level Psychology
Cara Flanagan

978 019 912962 1

Order your copies now

tel 01536 452620
fax 01865 313472

email schools.enquiries.uk@oup.com
web www.oxfordsecondary.co.uk/psychology

OXFORD
UNIVERSITY PRESS